Understanding

Hamlet

New and future titles in the Understanding Great Literature series include:

Understanding *The Catcher in the Rye*
Understanding *Flowers for Algernon*
Understanding *I Am the Cheese*
Understanding *The Outsiders*
Understanding *Romeo and Juliet*
Understanding *The Yearling*

Understanding

Hamlet

UNDERSTANDING GREAT LITERATURE

Don Nardo

Lucent Books
P.O. Box 289011
San Diego, CA 92198-9011

On Cover: *Hamlet and Horatio in the Churchyard* by
Eugene Delacroix.

Library of Congress Cataloging-in-Publication Data

Nardo, Don, 1947–
  Hamlet / by Don Nardo.
    p. cm. — (Understanding great literature)
  Includes bibliographical references and index.
  Summary: Discusses the play "Hamlet" by William Shakespeare,
including: performance history, story, and characters.
  ISBN 1-56006-830-2
  1. Shakespeare, William, 1564–1616. Hamlet—Juvenile
literature. [1. Shakespeare, William, 1564–1616. Hamlet. 2.
English literature—History and criticism.] I. Title. II. Series.
  PR2807 .N37 2001
  822.3'3—dc21

                          00-010556

Contents

"Except for a living man, there is nothing more wonderful than a book!" wrote the widely respected
nineteenth-century teacher and writer Charles
Kingsley. A book, he continued, "is a message to us from human
souls we never saw. And yet these [books] arouse us, terrify us,
teach us, comfort us, open our hearts to us as brothers." There
are many different kinds of books, of course; and Kingsley was
referring mainly to those containing literature—novels, plays,
short stories, poems, and so on. In particular, he had in mind
those works of literature that were and remain widely popular
with readers of all ages and from many walks of life.

Such popularity might be based on one or several factors. On
the one hand, a book might be read and studied by people in
generation after generation because it is a literary classic, with
characters and themes of universal relevance and appeal. Homer's
epic poems, the *Iliad* and the *Odyssey*, Chaucer's *Canterbury
Tales*, Shakespeare's *Hamlet* and *Romeo and Juliet*, and
Dickens's *A Christmas Carol* fall into this category. Some popular books, on the other hand, are more controversial. Mark
Twain's *Huckleberry Finn* and J. D. Salinger's *The Catcher in the
Rye*, for instance, have their legions of devoted fans who see them
as great literature; while others view them as less than worthy
because of their racial depictions, profanity, or other factors.

Still another category of popular literature includes realistic
modern fiction, including novels such as Robert Cormier's *I
Am the Cheese* and S. E. Hinton's *The Outsiders*. Their keen
social insights and sharp character portrayals have consistently

reached out to and captured the imaginations of many teenagers and young adults; and for this reason they are often assigned and studied in schools.

These and other similar works have become the "old standards" of the literary scene. They are the ones that people most often read, discuss, and study; and each has, by virtue of its content, critical success, or just plain longevity, earned the right to be the subject of a book examining its content. (Some, of course, like the *Iliad* and *Hamlet*, have been the subjects of numerous books already; but their literary stature is so lofty that there can never be too many books about them!) For millions of readers and students in one generation after another, each of these works becomes, in a sense, an adventure in appreciation, enjoyment, and learning.

The main purpose of Lucent's Understanding Great Literature series is to aid the reader in that ongoing literary adventure. Each volume in the series focuses on a single literary work that a majority of critics and teachers view as a classic and/or that is widely studied and discussed in schools. A typical volume first tells why the work in question is important. Then follow detailed overviews of the author's life, the work's historical background, its plot, its characters, and its themes. Numerous quotes from the work, as well as by critics and other experts, are interspersed throughout and carefully documented with footnotes for those who wish to pursue further research. Also included is a list of ideas for essays and other student projects relating to the work, an appendix of literary criticisms and analyses by noted scholars, and a comprehensive annotated bibliography.

The great nineteenth-century American poet Henry David Thoreau once quipped: "Read the best books first, or you may not have a chance to read them at all." For those who are reading or about to read the "best books" in the literary canon, the comprehensive, thorough, and thoughtful volumes of the Understanding Great Literature series are indispensable guides and sources of enrichment.

Hamlet Never Rests

Hamlet, the "melancholy Dane" created some four hundred years ago by English playwright William Shakespeare, never seems to slow down, much less to stop and rest. The fact is, somewhere in the world today, as has happened many thousands of times before and will happen countless times hereafter, a curtain is rising on a new performance of *Hamlet*. Some of those in the audience have seen the play before. But many are attending for the first time; let us call them *Hamlet* initiates. Regardless of the quality of the production, after the curtain falls the initiates will invariably walk away stamped with an indelible memory, one that will color, by way of comparison, any and all live or filmed productions of the play they may see later. That is part of the enduring power of this remarkable work, which many critics have called the greatest play ever written by the greatest playwright who ever lived.

Even if this last statement is an exaggeration, the play's unmatched record of performances and avalanche of literary and artistic interpretations demonstrate that it is surely the most *popular* play ever written. Indeed, since it was first staged in London in about 1600, *Hamlet* has been the world's most often performed play. It has attracted the greatest actors of each succeeding generation, all drawn by the beauty and emotional power of the lines and the challenge of discovering what makes the complex title character tick. "You can play it and play it as many times as opportunity occurs," stated the great stage and film actor Sir Laurence Olivier, "and still not get to the bottom of its box of wonders. . . . Once you have played it, it will devour you and obsess you for the rest of your life."[1] A more recent stage Hamlet, Stephen Berkoff, more concisely quipped, "In every actor is a Hamlet struggling to get out."[2]

A good many of the *Hamlet* initiates in the audiences watching these actors became equally hooked on the play. Widely respected British actor and Shakespearean scholar Michael Pennington remembers that his initial *Hamlet* experience, as it was for numerous others, was Olivier's renowned 1948 film of the play. This visually brooding, energetically staged and acted work won the Academy Award for best picture of the year (as well as one for Olivier as best actor in the title role). Since then, Pennington has seen scores of Hamlets and has also played Hamlet on several occasions. And yet, he says, "When I think of Hamlet, I still think of Olivier, because he was my first." The atmospheric black-and-white photography remains unforgettable, Pennington recalls. "This was done to save money, but was thought to reflect the bleak northern [European] tones of the play, which in fact it did." Most of all, Pennington remembers being mesmerized by the ghost of Hamlet's dead father, "a billowing amoebic [irregularly formed] figure, its face . . . obscure, its heart thumping in the battlement mists."[3]

That Olivier's version of *Hamlet* remains in a way Pennington's favorite is not surprising. "Most people's favorite Hamlets are their first experiences of the play," comments the renowned British actor Sir Alec Guinness, "which means they are probably young and it is to the young (with questioning minds) that the character [most] appeals."[4] In fact, Pennington was only thirteen when he saw Olivier's film. At the time, like other impressionable young people, he thought that the great actor's specific line readings, gestures, and general approach to the part constituted *the* way to play Hamlet and that this must be precisely the way Shakespeare had intended it. But later, Pennington learned that this was

The great English stage and screen actor Laurence Olivier as Hamlet in his award-winning 1948 film of the play.

only one of a seemingly endless number of ways to approach this mammoth and often mysterious role. Actors, directors, and scholars continue to argue (and likely always will) about the character's personality and motivations.

Why, for instance, when Hamlet suspects that his uncle has killed his father to marry his mother, does he not act immediately and decisively? Does he truly love his girlfriend, Ophelia, or is he only using her? When reciting the famous "To be or not to be" speech, is he actually contemplating suicide, or just venting his frustrations? Does he have repressed sexual feelings for his mother, Queen Gertrude? Does he really go mad, or is he just faking it? Everyone who approaches Hamlet has his or her own answers to these and other such questions. Collectively, they make up what scholars frequently refer to as the "Hamlet problem," which hovers perpetually and menacingly over the role and inevitably haunts all those who endeavor to play it. Thus, there are as many different interpretations of Hamlet and his dilemma as there are productions of the play. And there will always be new *Hamlet* initiates, both onstage and watching from the audience, to ponder and offer fresh solutions for the Hamlet problem. That is just one of the reasons that Hamlet never rests.

CHAPTER ONE

The Life, Times, and Works of William Shakespeare

T he number of words and lines that have been written about William Shakespeare and his works is so immense that if they were placed end to end they would encircle the earth several times. One might understandably ask, therefore, if all that could be said on him has already been said? The answer to that question would be a resounding "no." The words and lines that follow, along with those in countless works yet to be written about Shakespeare, are completely warranted because of the uniqueness and sheer enormity of his genius.

There are, of course, different kinds of genius. What was the nature of that possessed by Shakespeare? And what made him so unusual? It was decidedly not his originality, for he borrowed the plots and many of the themes of his plays from prior or contemporary literature and writers. He certainly had an uncommon gift for using the written word as a means of expression. Yet a fair number of other writers have displayed this gift as well as he. It was, rather, "the nature of his factual knowledge and the uses to which he put it," suggest noted Shakespearean scholars Gareth and Barbara Lloyd Evans. "The difference between his genius and that of most others is that he recognized and respected the trivia of his contemporaries as the truest source to feed his poetic imagination."[5] In other words, in addition to great writing ability, Shakespeare had an incredibly keen eye and memory for the details of people and their everyday lives.

Indeed, no other writer in human history has managed to capture the feelings, longings, strengths, frailties, triumphs, and tragedies of human beings and their lives so truthfully, in such detail, and on so grand a scale as Shakespeare. Character after character leaps up from his pages. Each seems just right for the time and place depicted in the work, yet at the same time, the character and his or her feelings and problems transcend that particular locale and age and hauntingly remind us of ourselves and people we have known. Because Shakespeare's characters are and will always remain timeless, universal, and part of the human condition, people will never cease to be drawn to him—as both a person and an artist—and to wonder what made him tick.

His Life Mysterious and Undocumented?

The exact details of Shakespeare's life, especially his early years, are unknown. Yet the often-voiced notion that the great playwright led a mysterious and undocumented life is a misconception. (This misconception has helped to fuel numerous vain attempts over the years to prove that someone else wrote his plays. The claimants include writers Francis Bacon, Ben Jonson, and John Donne, and several aristocrats, among them the earl of Southampton, Cardinal Wolsey, and even Queen Elizabeth herself. However, no convincing proof exists that any of these people secretly penned his works.) As the Evanses somewhat wittily put it:

> One of the most common pleas of the skeptical [person] is that what is known about Shakespeare's life could easily be written on one side of a small postcard, with room to spare. Invariably, those who urge this have no knowledge of the extent, nature, or whereabouts of documentary material relating to his life. If they did, they would find it necessary to purchase an extra consignment of postcards.[6]

This memorial bust in Stratford's Holy Trinity Church, where Shakespeare is buried, may be one of the few accurate depictions of the playwright.

In fact, for a common person of the Elizabethan period (spanning the late 1500s and early 1600s) Shakespeare's life was unusually well documented. The evidence consists of over one hundred official documents, including entries about him and his relatives in parish registers and town archives, legal records involving property transfers, and business letters to or about him. There are also more than fifty allusions to him and his works in the published writings of his contemporaries. These sources do not tell us much about Shakespeare's personality, likes and dislikes, and personal beliefs. Yet they provide enough information to piece together a concise outline of the important events of his life.

Shakespeare was born in 1564 in Stratford, now called Stratford-on-Avon, a village in Warwickshire County in central England. The exact day is somewhat uncertain, but tradition accepts it as April 23. If this date is indeed correct, it is an unusual coincidence, for April 23 is celebrated in England as St. George's Day, in honor of the country's patron saint, and is also the documented month and day of Shakespeare's own death fifty-two years later.[7]

A Crucial Historical Era

Much more important is the fact that Shakespeare came into the world during a particularly crucial historical era—the last decades of the sixteenth century—and in what was then one of the world's most pivotal nations—England. As it happened, this was one of the richest, most dynamic, and most opportune cultural and professional settings for aspiring poets and dramatists in all of Western history. Many great writers, among them Francis Bacon, Christopher Marlowe, Ben Jonson, and John Donne, were all born within a dozen years of Shakespeare's birth and published works during his lifetime. Writing plays was then, for the first time in England's history, coming to be seen as a legitimate art form, as evidenced partly by the construction of England's first public theater when Shakespeare was twelve.

Moreover, Shakespeare was born in a time when powerful European nations like England were greatly expanding their horizons. It was "an era of change and restlessness," remarks Shakespearean scholar Karl Holzknecht.

> Everywhere—in religion, in philosophy, in politics, in science, in literature—new ideas were springing into life and coming into conflict with the established order of things. . . . A whole series of events and discoveries, coming together at the end of the fifteenth century [just preceding the Elizabethan age], transformed . . . many of the institutions and the habits of mind that we

call medieval. The gradual break-up of feudalism . . . the discovery of gunpowder and . . . the mariner's compass and the possibility of safely navigating the limitless ocean, the production of paper and the invention of printing, and . . . the Copernican system of astronomy which formulated a new center of the universe—all of these new conceptions had a profound effect upon human thought and became the foundations for intellectual, moral, social, and economic changes which quickly made themselves felt.[8]

In addition to these forces that shaped Europe in the 1500s, there were several important events that occurred in England during Shakespeare's own lifetime. Perhaps the most renowned of these occurred in 1588, when the English defeated the huge Spanish Armada (an event that saved England from invasion and foreign occupation). Not long afterward, Sir Francis Drake, Sir John Hawkins, and other adventurous English sea captains helped to turn the sea lanes into great highways for England's growing naval power. And in 1607, when Shakespeare was about forty-three, English settlers founded the colony of Jamestown in Virginia, giving England a foothold in the New World.

England's command of the waves brought it commercial success, and its ports and cities became bustling centers of high finance, social life, and the arts. Amid all of this, the theater, increasingly recognized as an art form, provided a fertile, creative atmosphere for the efforts and innovations of ambitious young playwrights like William Shakespeare.

Shakespeare's Education

It was by no means evident at first that young Will Shakespeare would turn out to be a major contributor to and shaper of this new and growing theater world. When he was born, his father, John Shakespeare, was a glover and perhaps also a wool and leather dealer in Stratford. The town was far away from the bustling, cosmopolitan London, where most actors, writers, and other artists congregated and worked. The elder Shakespeare also held various local community positions, among them ale taster, town councilman, town treasurer, and eventually bailiff (mayor). John and his wife, Mary Arden, were married shortly before the accession of Queen Elizabeth I to the English throne in 1558, and they subsequently produced eight children, of whom William was the third child and eldest son.

It is fairly certain that from age seven to about age sixteen Shakespeare attended the town grammar school. There, students studied Latin grammar and literature, including the works of the Roman writers Terence, Cicero, Virgil, and Ovid, as well as works by later European authors such as the Dutch moralist Erasmus. Following the educational customs of the day, Shakespeare and his classmates had to memorize grammar and other information and then repeat it back when drilled by the schoolmaster. A rough idea of the process is afforded in this scene from Shakespeare's *The Merry Wives of Windsor*, in which a parson (Evans) tests the Latin knowledge of a young boy (Will, a name unlikely to have been chosen by chance):

EVANS: What is your genitive case plural, William?

WILL: Genitive case?

EVANS: Ay.

WILL: *Horum, harum, horum.* . . .

EVANS: Show me now, William, your declension of your pronouns.

WILL: Forsooth [in truth], I have forgot.

EVANS: It is *qui, quae, quod*: if you forget your *qui*'s, your *quae*'s, and your *quod*'s, you must be preeches [whipped].[9]

In addition to these formal studies, Shakespeare must have done much reading on his own time in his teens and twenties.

We know this partly because his works reveal a knowledge not only of Latin but of French and several other languages. Shakespeare was also well versed in both ancient and recent European history and fiction as well, including the classic works of Italy's Boccaccio and England's Chaucer. In addition, and perhaps most important, Shakespeare amassed a huge body of practical knowledge about life. In fact, says Shakespearean scholar John F. Andrews,

> Judging from his plays and poems, we may infer that Shakespeare was interested in virtually every aspect of human life—in professions such as law, medicine, religion, and teaching; in everyday occupations such as farming, sheepherding, tailoring, and shopkeeping; in skills such as fishing, gardening, and cooking. Much of what Shakespeare knew about these and countless other subjects he would have acquired from books. He must have been a voracious reader. But he would have learned a great deal, also, from simply being alert to all that went on around him.[10]

By his young adulthood, therefore, Shakespeare possessed an impressive, highly rounded education, most of it self-taught.

Why Did Shakespeare Go into the Theater?

Informed conjecture about his childhood and education aside, the first certain fact about Shakespeare after his birth was his wedding, which his marriage license dates as November 27, 1582. His bride, Anne Hathaway, was the daughter of a farmer from the nearby village of Shottery. She was eight years older than he. Local documents also reveal a daughter, Susanna, christened May 26, 1583, and twins, Hamnet and Judith, christened February 26, 1585. Other surviving records show that Hamnet died in 1596 at the age of eleven.

The exact reason that young Will Shakespeare chose the theater as a profession is unknown, but certain facts help us form an educated guess. Among these is the fact that traveling companies of actors visited and performed at Stratford periodically. For instance, Stratford records indicate such visits from the theatrical troupes the Queen's Men and the Earl of Worcester's Men in 1568 and 1569, when Shakespeare was about five. These companies presented the most popular plays of the day on makeshift wooden stages, described here by noted scholar A. A. Mendilow:

Before 1576, there were no permanent theaters in existence in England. . . . All stage performances for public entertainment in the larger towns before and even after 1576 were conducted on movable platforms . . . covering a curtained lower story where the actors could change their costumes; the entry from below to the upper acting area could also serve as a "hell-mouth" into which the wicked were thrown in the old religious drama. The platform was open on all four sides as a rule, and perhaps had a canopy against the rain. . . . The whole cart was on wheels and constituted a traveling theater which could be set up in market squares and open spaces. In Shakespeare's time, companies of actors still traveled in the provinces, especially when performances were forbidden in London because of an outbreak of the plague.[11]

It may well be that traveling productions like these fascinated the young Shakespeare enough to inspire his going to London to try his luck in the theater, an event that likely occurred in 1587, the year before the English victory over the Spanish Armada.

Various undocumented stories have survived about the young man's first professional job. One maintains that he tended horses outside the Globe Theater until offered the position of assistant prompter. Regarding this contention, the Evanses write,

> There are two objections to this sturdy, ubiquitous [existing seemingly everywhere] story. The first is that there is no evidence whatsoever, and the second is that the Globe Theater was not built until 1599—ten years at least after Shakespeare arrived in London. . . . [There exists the] possibility that he looked after horses at some other theater and that, after all, the early attachments of many of our eminent dramatists to their chosen profession have been no less menial.[12]

"Another theory seems more likely," writes Shakespearean scholar François Laroque, namely that

> Shakespeare attached himself to a theatrical company—perhaps the Queen's Men, which happened to have lost one of its members in a brawl. The young Shakespeare could easily have stepped into his shoes, as experience was not required. Actors learned on the job.[13]

His Reputation Begins to Grow

However Shakespeare actually entered the theater, once he did so there is little doubt that the observant and talented young man learned quicker than most. By 1593 he had written *Richard III*, *The Comedy of Errors*, and *Henry VI, Parts 1, 2, and 3*, earning him a solid reputation as a playwright and actor in the London theater scene. At first, he did not attach himself exclusively to any specific theatrical company, but worked on and off with several, including that of Richard Burbage, the finest and most acclaimed actor of the time. Burbage, four years younger than Shakespeare, became the playwright's close friend and colleague and eventually played the title roles in the original productions of some of his greatest plays, including *Hamlet, Richard III, King Lear,* and *Othello.*

During most of 1593 and 1594, London's theaters were closed because of a severe outbreak of the plague, and Shakespeare temporarily channeled his energies into writing poetry. Two long poems, *Venus and Adonis* and *Lucrece,* the only works he ever published himself, were completed in this interval and dedicated to the earl of Southampton. The earl was a close friend who, some evidence suggests, lent the playwright money when he needed it. These works established Shakespeare as an accepted and respectable literary figure, whereas his plays, like those of other playwrights of the time, were viewed as popular but low-brow entertainment rather than as legitimate literature.

It may have been one of Southampton's loans (or perhaps an outright gift) that enabled Shakespeare to buy a modest share of a new theatrical company—the Lord Chamberlain's Men. Its founding in 1594 marked an important turning point in the playwright's career. Performing at all the major theaters of the day, including the Theatre, the Swan, and the Curtain (the famous Globe had not yet been built), the company thereafter provided Shakespeare with a ready creative outlet for his plays as well as a regular income. By 1603, when it became known as the King's Servants, it was performing periodically at the royal court and Shakespeare was a major shareholder in all company profits.

Plays of Astonishing Variety and Quality

As a permanent member of the company, Shakespeare had the opportunity to work with the best English actors of the day on a regular basis. In addition to the great Burbage, the actors included Henry Condell, John Heminge, William Sly, and Will Kempe. Kempe, one of the great comic players of the Elizabethan stage, specialized in broad, slapstick comedy and physical clowning. Evidence suggests that he played the role of Peter, the bumbling servant to the Nurse in *Romeo and Juliet*, and Dogberry, the constable in *Much Ado About Nothing*. Over the years Shakespeare wrote a number of comic roles especially for Kempe, among them Costard in *Love's Labor's Lost*, Launce in *The Two Gentlemen of Verona*, and Bottom in *A Midsummer Night's Dream*.

Indeed, from 1594 on, Shakespeare devoted most of his time to writing plays, turning out a large number of astonishing variety and quality between 1594 and 1601. A partial list includes the comedies *The Taming of the Shrew*, *The Two Gentlemen of Verona*, *The Merry Wives of Windsor*, and *Twelfth Night*; the histories *Richard II*, *Henry IV*, *Parts 1 and 2*, and *Henry V*; and the tragedies *Romeo and Juliet*, *Julius Caesar*, and *Hamlet*. Not surprisingly, the playwright's reputation soared, as evidenced by this 1598 remembrance by schoolmaster Francis Meres (died 1647), praising his talent and skills:

> The sweet witty soul of [the great ancient Roman poet] Ovid lives in mellifluous [smooth and sweet] and honey-tongued Shakespeare, witness his *Venis and Adonis*, his *Lucrece*, his . . . sonnets. . . . As [the Roman playwrights] Plautus and Seneca are accounted the best for Comedy and Tragedy among the Latins: so Shakespeare among the English is the most excellent in both kinds for the stage.[14]

Even in the midst of turning out so many masterpieces, the playwright somehow managed to find the time for journeys back and forth to rural Stratford and the family and community obligations centered there. In 1597 he became a local burgess, or council member, by buying New Place, the largest and finest home in the town (the property included two barns and two gardens). Town records show that he later bought other property in the area, confirming that he had by now acquired more than what was then viewed as a comfortable living.

The Globe Theater and Its Stage

It is probable that a significant portion of this large income must have come from Shakespeare's one-eighth share in the profits of the new and very successful Globe Theater, which opened in 1599. He and his colleagues in the Lord Chamberlain company had found it difficult to renew their lease at the Theatre playhouse and had decided to build their own playhouse. In the short span of eight months they built the Globe on the south side of the Thames River and entered into a joint ownership deal with Sir Nicholas Brend, who owned the property. This marked the first known instance in theatrical history of actors owning the theater in which they performed. It was for this theater and the specific properties of its stage that Shakespeare tailored the plays he wrote in the years that followed. Shakespearean scholar Ronald Watkins, an expert on Elizabethan theaters, provides this informative description of the Globe in its heyday:

The [building's] octagonal frame is about 84 feet in outside diameter—hardly more than the length of a lawn-tennis court. A concentric octagon within the frame bounds the Yard, which is open to the sky. Between the two octagons the space is roofed and the building rises to three stories. Nearly five of the eight sides of the octagonal frame are occupied by galleries from which the eyes of the spectators converge upon the stage. The Yard will hold 600 standing close-packed (the groundlings); the three galleries about 1,400. . . . Intimacy [between actors and audience] is possible at the Globe because of the position of the Platform [i.e., the stage]. The middle point of the front edge is the exact center of the octagon. The actor . . . can have his audience on three sides of him. There is real distance in the depth of the stage, and an actor in the Study [or discovery space, the small area, often curtained, at the rear

A detail from a 1616 engraving shows the octagonal Globe Theater, where many of Shakespeare's plays premiered.

of the stage] will seem remote while another in front seems close at hand; this contrast in their relation to the audience is often used for dramatic purpose. The Platform is the main field of action for the players. . . . It tapers towards the front, stands probably between 4 and 5 feet from the floor of the Yard, and is protected from the groundlings by rails; the front edge is 24 feet wide, at its widest it is 41 feet; its depth from front to Study-curtain is 29 feet; and the Study itself, when open, adds a further 7 or 8 feet. Conspicuous towards the front of the Platform stand the two pillars supporting the . . . Heavens [a roof-like canopy overhanging the middle of the stage]. . . . The Tiring-house [containing dressing rooms for the actors] is the permanent background to the platform; its back is turned to the afternoon sun, so that no freaks of light and shade distract from the illusion [since the plays were presented in the afternoon]. . . . On the Platform level the . . . Study is flanked by two doors . . . the two main entries for the players.[15]

Between 1600 and 1607, the Globe's open-air yard and platform were the scene of the premieres of most of what are now viewed as Shakespeare's greatest tragedies: *Hamlet*, *Othello*, *King Lear*, *Macbeth*, and *Antony and Cleopatra*.

His Final Years and Honors

Shakespeare survived the writing of these superb and timeless works by only eight years. Apparently now secure in his fame and fortune, he seems to have spent much of his time during these years at New Place in Stratford. There, according to various entries in local records and diaries, he became increasingly involved in community and family affairs. He still wrote plays, but no longer at the rapid pace he had maintained in his youth. His last works included *Coriolanus, Pericles, The Winter's Tale, Henry VIII*, and *The Two Noble Kinsmen*, all first performed between 1608 and 1613. *Kinsmen* turned out to be his swan song. He must have become seriously ill in March 1616, for his will was executed on March 25. He died nearly a month later on April 23. The bulk of his estate went to his wife, sister, and daughters Susanna and Judith, although he also left money to some of his theater colleagues, including Richard Burbage.

A few years after Shakespeare's death, a monument to him, designed by prosperous stonemason Gheerart (or Gerard) Janssen, was erected in Stratford Church. According to University of Maryland scholar Samuel Schoenbaum,

Janssen worked mainly in white marble, with black for the two Corinthian columns, and black touchstone for the inlaid panels. The columns support a cornice [horizontal molding] on which sit two small cherubic figures, both male; the left one, holding a spade, represents Labor; the right, with a skull and inverted torch, signifies Rest. They flank the familiar Shakespearean [coat of] arms, helm, and crest, carved in bas-relief on a square stone block. The design forms a pyramid at the apex [top] of which sits another skull. . . . Wearing a sleeveless gown over a doublet, Shakespeare stands with a quill pen in his right hand, a sheet of paper under his left, both hands resting on a cushion.[16]

Shakespeare received a greater posthumous honor in 1623 when two of his former theatrical partners, Henry Condell and John Heminge, published the so-called First Folio, a collection of the playwright's complete plays, under the title *Mr. William Shakespeare's Comedies, Histories, & Tragedies. Published According to the True Original Copies.* The exact nature of these "copies" that served as the folio's basis remains unclear. Most scholars assume that they were various "quartos," early printed versions of the plays, which the actors often used as performance scripts.

Whatever its sources, the First Folio was extremely important to posterity because it included eighteen plays that had not already been printed in quarto form and that might otherwise have been lost forever. Among them were some of the playwright's greatest works—*As You Like It, Macbeth, Antony and Cleopatra, The Tempest,* and the great political play *Julius Caesar.* These works, along with Shakespeare's other plays, have been "accorded a place in our culture above and beyond their topmost place in our literature," writes Harvard University scholar Harry Levin.

> They have been virtually canonized as humanistic scriptures, the tested residue of pragmatic [practical] wisdom, a general collection of quotable texts and usable examples. Reprinted, reedited, commented upon, and translated into most languages, they have preempted more space on the library shelves than the books of—or about—any other author. Meanwhile, they have become a staple of the school and college curricula, as well as the happiest of hunting grounds for scholars and critics.[17]

Probably the "happiest hunting ground" of all, for students, scholars, and critics alike, is also the most popular of Shakespeare's plays—*Hamlet.*

CHAPTER TWO

The Original Sources and Performance History of *Hamlet*

In a sense, Shakespeare's *Hamlet* and its title character are living, breathing entities that change and evolve over time. First, contrary to popular belief, the text itself is not fixed and unchangeable, with all of its words and lines "written in stone." Rather, it is quite flexible, as evidenced by the fact that no two individual productions are exactly the same in content and length. This is partly because at least three versions of the play existed in Shakespeare's time. Ever since then, producers and directors have regularly combined sections from the three texts in various ways and deleted other sections at will, creating countless different and unique textual versions. Certain core events and speeches are always retained, however. For example, in every production of the play, whether on stage or screen, Hamlet encounters the ghost of his dead father, recites the "To be or not to be" speech, mutters "Alas, poor Yorick" while holding a human skull, and dies of a dose of poison following an exciting, climactic sword fight.

Another important factor that makes each new production of *Hamlet* unique is that actors and directors invariably attempt to develop their own personalized interpretations of the lines and character motivations and to search for fresh approaches in costuming and staging. There have been moody Hamlets, angry ones, weak ones, strong ones, crafty ones, athletic ones, clumsy ones, noble ones, neurotic ones, and all manner of others, some possessing complex combinations of several of these traits. The play's staging has been no less varied. All manner of settings, from real castles to bare stages, have been employed, as well as a wide array of time periods and dress styles ranging from medieval to modern day. This extremely varied performance history has given rise to the popular notion that there are as many different Hamlets as there are actors itching to play the role.

It is equally revealing that the existence of multiple Hamlets, each stressing certain and often distinct themes and characteristics, is not just a post-Shakespearean phenomenon. In fact, several earlier versions of Hamlet's troubles and adventures at the Danish royal court long predated Shakespeare's play. And there is no doubt that at least some of these stories and plays influenced him in structuring the characters, plot, and themes of his own version. The following questions are crucial: Which of these early sources did Shakespeare have access to? How much did he borrow from these sources (and conversely, how much of his version is original)? Why did he stress certain themes over others, in particular the motifs of murder and revenge?

Over the years, Shakespearean and literary scholars have churned out hundreds of books, essays, and articles discussing and answering these questions. Though some still disagree about a few of the details, a general consensus has emerged about the play's sources and background. (Of course, no such consensus exists about how to stage it and play the lead role. This means that it will surely continue to evolve, finding new meanings and relevance for future generations of people in diverse cultures.)

The Revenge Play Tradition

The question of why Shakespeare placed so much emphasis on the themes of murder and revenge is fairly easy to answer. When he wrote *Hamlet*, about the year 1600, he intended it to exploit a theatrical genre that had recently become very popular in London and other English cities—the "revenge play." A typical revenge play portrayed a hero seeking bloody justice for the wrongful acts of one or more "villains" and followed a specific formula, as described here by noted Shakespearean scholar Norrie Epstein:

> Most of the play consists of the hero's plot to avenge an injustice or a crime committed against a family member. In their obsession with family honor and the violent means they'll take to preserve it, the characters of a revenge play resemble the tightly knit Corleone family in *The Godfather*. A rape, a dismemberment, or an act of incest might add sensationalism, and often a ghost incites the avenger to do his bloody business. By the last act, the stage is usually littered with carnage—much to everyone's delight.[18]

Other typical elements of revenge plays included the leading male character disguising himself or feigning insanity as part of his scheme to achieve vengeance, and the leading female character going mad and dying of grief. Among the best and most popular revenge plays that preceded *Hamlet* are *The Spanish Tragedy* (ca. 1586), by English playwright Thomas Kyd, and Shakespeare's own *Titus Andronicus* (1593).

Still, though *Hamlet* certainly falls into this revenge play tradition, it does not simply follow the tired old formula slavishly and unimaginatively, like so many other works in the genre did. Indeed, assert Shakespearean scholars Phyllis Abrahms and Alan Brody,

> *Hamlet* is a masterpiece not because it conforms to a set of conventions but because it takes those conventions and transmutes them into the pure gold of vital, relevant meaning. Hamlet's feigned madness, for instance, becomes the touchstone [noteworthy example] for an illumination of the mysterious nature of sanity itself.[19]

The Playwright's Sources

Just as Shakespeare did not invent the revenge play and its peculiar literary and theatrical conventions, neither did he invent the main characters and basic plot of his own revenge play *Hamlet*. Most commonly, he borrowed his plots and leading characters from existing sources, including ancient myths, historical accounts, popular stories, poems, novels, and so on. And *Hamlet* was no exception.

One of the playwright's sources for *Hamlet* may have been the *Historia Danica* ("Chronicles of the Danish Realm"). This Latin work, by the twelfth-century Danish historian Saxo Grammaticus, tells about a medieval Danish prince named Amlethus.[20] While the prince is still a child, his uncle, Fengon, murders the king, Amlethus's father, and marries the queen, Gerutha. The boy soon becomes obsessed with getting revenge. But because he is still young and relatively powerless, he bides his time, all the while pretending to have gone mad in order to keep his uncle from discovering his plans for retribution. Nevertheless, Fengon suspects Amlethus is only feigning madness and tries, unsuccessfully, to trick him into lowering his guard. Eventually, the young man sets fire to the castle's great hall and kills Fengon with the usurper's own sword.

Though scholars are not absolutely certain that Shakespeare had access to this early Danish work, it is almost certain that he was familiar with a 1576 French story based on it. The French version, which retained many of the characters and events of the original, appeared as one of several tales in the *Histories Tragiques*, by François de Belleforest. (Belleforest's work was translated into English by Thomas Pavier as *The Hystorie of Hamblet* in 1608, about seven or eight years after Shakespeare wrote his own version; but Shakespeare may have read the story in the original French sometime in the 1580s or 1590s.) "Many of the essential elements of the [Hamlet] tragedy" can be found here, points out G. R. Hibbard, a former professor of English at the University of Waterloo in Ontario.

[These elements include] the single combat between old Hamlet [Hamlet's father] and the king of Norway; the seduction of Gertrude [Hamlet's mother] by Claudius [Hamlet's uncle]; the murder of old Hamlet; Claudius's marriage to Gertrude; the son's duty to avenge his father; his counterfeiting madness [and so on]. . . . To the central figure, Belleforest contributed far more than bare bones. He offered Shakespeare the ruthlessly efficient avenger of Saxo's story made more complex by a streak of melancholy in his nature.[21]

At first glance, it would appear that Shakespeare was heavily indebted to Belleforest. However, it is difficult to tell just how much came from this French version of the story. On the one hand, while there are many similarities between the two works, there are just as many differences. Also, other writers utilized the same plot and characters in the sixteenth century, and Shakespeare had access to their works, each of which likely provided him with inspiration of one kind or another.

For example, a good many scholars are convinced that Shakespeare was especially influenced by one particular work based on the old Danish tale, a play that was performed often in the 1580s and 1590s but subsequently lost. This play, which may have been written by Thomas Kyd, author of *The Spanish Tragedy*, has come to be called the *Ur-Hamlet*. (The prefix "Ur" is a reference to the ancient Mesopotamian city of Ur, one of the first known human cities; its use in this manner denotes an "earlier" or "ancestral" version of something.) Because the play no longer exists, no one can say for sure exactly what and how much Shakespeare borrowed from it, but it is tantalizing to speculate. The fact is, the main character in his version is much more introspective and thoughtful and puts off enacting his revenge much longer than the Hamlets in the Danish and French versions. Were these enhancements, which gave the character so much added dimension, innovations of Shakespeare's? Or should they be credited to the author of the *Ur-Hamlet*? At present, these questions still cannot be answered with any certainty.[22]

Early Printed Versions and Performances

Luckily, scholars know quite a bit more about the earliest printed versions of Shakespeare's *Hamlet*, including the two quartos (printed performance scripts). It is important to emphasize that this play, like so many others written over the centuries, had, and still has, no single authorized text. "Indeed, the *Hamlet* we read today is not identical to any one of the three existing Renaissance printings of the play," explains Susanne L. Wofford of the University of Wisconsin at Madison.

It may well have been that such a single, stable text did not exist in the Globe Theater either. Like any drama company, Shakespeare's company probably added and cut scenes from plays when they went on the road or performed at court. So when a modern director decides to cut a speech or even moves it to a different part of the play, he or she may be treating the text of the play more in the way that Shakespeare and his company would have done than is a critic who challenges such practices. A play text is not like a modern lyric poem or a novel, for which there is a secure text, and the complications of printing history only exaggerate this point for the text of a Renaissance play like *Hamlet*.[23]

This printing history began with the First Quarto, which scholars often refer to using the abbreviation "Q1." It appeared in 1603 with the title *The Tragical History of Hamlet, Prince of Denmark, by William Shakespeare*, along with the added subtitle "As it hath been divers times acted by His Highness' servants in the city of London, as also in the two universities of Cambridge and Oxford and elsewhere." A good deal shorter than the later versions, the First Quarto is full of errors and most scholars have come to view it as unreliable; therefore they often refer to it as the "bad quarto." The consensus of opinion is that this corrupted version was reconstructed from memory by one or more actors who had been in a previous production of the play.

The Second Quarto of *Hamlet* (abbreviated "Q2"), which was first printed in 1604, is about twice as long as the first one. It bore a new subtitle: "Newly imprinted and enlarged to almost as much again as it was, according to the true and perfect copy." Because a majority of scholars suspect that said "perfect copy" was based directly on Shakespeare's own original manuscript, they usually refer to the Second Quarto as the "good quarto."

The third important early version of *Hamlet* appeared in the 1623 First Folio (abbreviated "F1") of the author's works. This one has some eighty-five lines not found in the Second Quarto, but the third version also lacks about two hundred of the good quarto's lines. Most modern editions of the play use various combinations of the Second Quarto and First Folio versions. (The differences among these early printed versions are not always just a matter of omissions and additions. Sometimes the actual wording is different. For example, the First Quarto begins the play's most famous speech with "To be or not to be, ay there's the point," as compared to the more familiar later version "To be or not to be, that is the question.")

As was the usual procedure at the time, a play's quartos were published well after the play had already been performed in public. The date of *Hamlet*'s first production is uncertain and might have been as early as 1598 or as late as 1602. The most likely period is 1600–1601, based partly on clues within the text itself. In act 2, scene 2, for example, Hamlet asks the courtier Rosencrantz why the actors visiting the castle are traveling around rather than appearing in their own theater. Rosencrantz asserts that professional actors are out of favor because of "an eyrie [nest] of children" who "berattle [berate] the common [public] stages." This is a direct reference to the so-called War of the Theaters, which took place between 1599 and 1601. During these years, private theaters using inexperienced child actors competed with and threatened the livelihoods of the more professional public playhouses like those in which Shakespeare worked.

The First Actors in the Title Role

Whenever it was that the first performance of *Hamlet* took place, there is no doubt about who played the title role in that seminal production. It was Shakespeare's friend and colleague Richard Burbage, who, by all accounts, was one of the greatest actors of the Elizabethan age. It is interesting to note that Burbage is said to have weighed some 235 pounds. This seems to corroborate the Queen's line in act 5, scene 2, in which, seeing her son dueling, she remarks, "He's fat and scant of breath." Over the centuries, however, most, if not all, Hamlets have been slim, so both actors and scholars have tended to interpret the line in question to mean "out of shape" or "out of practice," rather than physically plump. This is another example of the many ways textual and visual interpretations of the play change and evolve over time.

The list of actors who have succeeded Burbage in the much-coveted
role of Hamlet is a distinguished one.
Another great Elizabethan player,
Joseph Taylor, became the role's chief
interpreter when Burbage died in
1619. In 1663, Thomas Betterton
began playing Hamlet and continued
to do so until 1709, when he was in
his seventies. An August 1668 entry
in the journal of the noted English
diarist Samuel Pepys tells how he
went "to the Duke of York's playhouse, and saw 'Hamlet,' which we
have not seen this year before, or
more; and [we were] mightily pleased
with it, but above all with Betterton,
the best part, I believe, that ever man

*An early early seventeenth-
century rendering of Shakespeare's friend and colleague,
Elizabethan actor Richard
Burbage.*

acted."[24] A portrait of Betterton in the part, which still hangs in a
London theatrical club, shows him in the dark and somber attire
that thereafter became associated with the character.

The eighteenth century also had its share of notable
Hamlets. One of the greatest was David Garrick, who began
playing the part in 1742. His atmospheric performance is
described in a scene in Henry Fielding's 1749 novel *Tom Jones*,
in which the character Partridge comments, "If that little man
there upon the stage is not frightened [by his encounter with
the ghost], I never saw any man frightened in my life."[25] In
1783, another distinguished English actor, John Philip Kemble,
began playing Hamlet. His contribution to the role's interpre-
tive evolution was a heavy emphasis on the character's gloomi-
ness and madness. A contemporary German critic wrote of his
Hamlet: "What Kemble brought prominently out was the sad,
the melancholy, the noble suffering aspect of the character,
[while at the same time he] bore himself like a man of high

blood and breeding."[26] The English novelist Sir Walter Scott described Kemble as "the grave, studious, contemplative actor, who [im]personated Hamlet to the life."[27] The same century also witnessed the first important American Hamlet, Lewis Hallam, who presented the play in Philadelphia in 1759.

Following in this tradition, some powerful nineteenth-century American actors tackled the role of Hamlet. Among the greatest of the century was Edwin Booth (whose brother, John Wilkes Booth, also an actor, assassinated Abraham Lincoln). About Booth's stately performance, a reviewer for the *Atlantic Monthly* wrote in 1866:

> Where a burlier tragedian must elaborately pose himself for the youth he would assume, this actor so easily and constantly falls into beautiful attitudes and movements, that he seems to go about, as we heard a humorist say, "making statues all over the stage." No picture can equal the scene where Horatio and Marcellus swear by his sword, he holding the crossed hilt upright between the two, his head thrown back and lit with high resolve [emphasized to great effect].[28]

Other great nineteenth-century Hamlets included the renowned English actors Sir Henry Irving and Sir Johnston Forbes-Robertson.

Also in the 1900s, in one of the most controversial portrayals of the role in that or any period, was the famous actress Sarah Bernhardt. At the age of fifty-four, she appeared in an 1899 Paris production of *Hamlet*, receiving decidedly mixed reviews. Some critics curtly dismissed her effort, one of them saying that it was ridiculous for "an elderly lady encased in black silk tights"[29] to attempt to play Hamlet, which, he insisted, had clearly been written for a man. But other critics found much to admire in Bernhardt's portrayal. Since that time a considerable number of other women have assailed the role, among them the renowned Danish actress Asta Nielsen (in a silent film version of the play), Australian-born Dame Judith Anderson (perhaps most famous for her role as the sinister housekeeper in Alfred Hitchcock's *Rebecca*), and the gifted English stage actress and director Eva Le Gallienne.

Some Notable Twentieth-Century Hamlets

Many well-known actors carried the Hamlet performance tradition into the twentieth century, both onstage and in the new and powerful visual art form of film. One of the most acclaimed and probably the most influential Hamlet interpretation of the century was that of British actor John Gielgud, who first played the role at London's Old Vic Theater in

The renowned nineteenth-century American actor Edwin Booth, photographed in his Hamlet costume at the height of his career.

1929. Gielgud emphasized the Danish prince's nobility and restraint. His Hamlet was a sensitive, intellectual, introspective man who preferred to refrain from shouting and violent gestures. "Gielgud's view of the chief character," writes University of Arizona scholar Mary Z. Maher,

his mode of playing, and much of his stage business set the fashion for Hamlets in the decades to come. As a model for others, Gielgud cannot be overestimated. Here, indeed, was a definitive Hamlet. . . . It was a performance which combined highlighted theatrical moments with the psychological realism of an internally tormented man trapped in a web of circumstantial events. His tears . . . elicited pity and secured the compassion of his audience. . . . Gielgud truly was "the glass of fashion and the mold of form" through which modern Hamlets mirrored themselves.[30]

In 1964, Gielgud approached the play from another angle when he directed Richard Burton, another memorable Hamlet, in a long-running and generally well-received New York production. Burton, known for his expressive baritone voice and intense acting style, played the role as a sometimes angry but also often bewildered and frustrated man caught in circumstances he could not control. This production is perhaps most notable in that it featured two of the world's greatest actors teaming up in an attempt to unravel the mysteries of the world's greatest acting role.[31]

Richard Burton poses with his sword during rehearsals for the 1964 Broadway production of Hamlet.

Other notable twentieth-century Hamlets included Maurice Evans, John Barrymore, Alec Guinness, Laurence Olivier (in London in 1937 and in the 1948 film), David Warner, Christopher Plummer (in a 1964 TV production shot on location at Elsinore in Denmark), Nicol Williamson (in the 1969 film), Mel Gibson (in the 1990 film), and Kenneth Branagh (in the 1997 film). Each of these actors brought his own unique talents, physical bearing, and personal ideas for interpretation to the role. There is no doubt that in the future other distinguished actors will do the same, continuing to shape and reshape, examine and reexamine, and take apart and put back together this amazingly flexible and compelling work.

CHAPTER THREE

The Story Told in Shakespeare's *Hamlet*

In 1935 noted scholar and critic John Dover Wilson published *What Happens in Hamlet*, one of the most famous and important books ever written about Shakespeare's *Hamlet*. Wilson's concern in the work is to explain the title character's problems and motivations, not to summarize the plot. But adding a question mark to the title of the book creates a question—what happens in *Hamlet?*—that some of those who are unfamiliar with the play would like answered more literally.

Before answering that question, however, it is helpful to examine briefly the setting and background events. The action of the play takes place at Elsinore, Denmark's royal castle, a sprawling structure of massive, somber stones, topped by ancient battlements and containing many rooms and just as many secrets. The time period is not specified, but it is probable that Shakespeare envisioned it as late medieval times. (Of course, in performance the play can be and often is set in other periods, including the modern era.)

As for the events leading up to the story, Denmark's former ruler, old King Hamlet, recently died, leaving behind his wife, Queen Gertrude, and son, Prince Hamlet. The prince was away at school. Shortly after his return to Elsinore, less than two months after his father's passing, his mother shocked him by marrying his uncle, Claudius. Ever since, the young man has been wearing black, not only to mourn the dead king, but also to show his displeasure with the new royal union and what he views as the indecent haste in which it was consummated. Meanwhile, the threat of war looms. Fortinbras, a prince of the neighboring kingdom of Norway, is preparing to invade Denmark, hoping to recover property his father had earlier lost to old Hamlet.

Act One: The Ghost

The play opens on a dark winter night. As midnight nears, Horatio, one of young Hamlet's school friends who is visiting Elsinore, climbs to the top of the castle's battlements. There he meets with two sentries, Bernardo and Marcellus. In fearful whispers, they tell him that on each of the two preceding nights they have seen a ghostly apparition wandering along the battlements, a figure dressed in armor and looking very much like the deceased king, old Hamlet. At first, Horatio is skeptical. But suddenly the Ghost appears before them. "Look where it comes again!"[32] Marcellus cries. Horatio attempts to communicate with it, urging "By heaven I charge thee speak!"[33] But the frightening figure stalks away as suddenly as it had come, leaving the three men to ponder why the former king would come back to haunt the living. Eventually, the Ghost reappears to them. This time it seems about to speak, but then the cock crows (as dawn approaches) and it departs once more. Horatio decides that his friend, the prince, must be told about this singular apparition.

Later that morning, in the castle's audience chamber, Claudius and Gertrude hold court. The new king sends a message to Norway, hoping that war can be avoided by the use of diplomacy. Then Laertes, the young son of the court chamberlain, Polonius, requests permission to return to France, from where he had journeyed to attend Claudius's recent coronation ceremony. After granting Laertes' request, the king and queen turn to Hamlet, who, still dressed in black, has been sitting silently nearby. Gertrude tries to get her son to snap out of his gloomy mood. "Good Hamlet," she says, "cast thy nighted [black] color off. And let thine eye look like a friend on Denmark. Do not forever with vailed [downcast] lids seek for thy noble father in the dust."[34] But her words fail to change his mood. After the king, queen, and courtiers clear the hall, leaving Hamlet alone, the young man vents his anger and frustration at his mother's remarriage. "That it should come to this!" he hisses.

But two months dead—nay, not so much, not two! . . .

Oh God! A beast that wants [lacks] discourse of reason

Would have mourned longer—married with my uncle;

My father's brother, but no more like my father

Than I to Hercules. . . . It is not, nor it cannot come to good.[35]

At that moment, Hamlet is interrupted by Horatio, who enters followed by Marcellus and Bernardo. They tell him about their run-in with the Ghost and he agrees to keep watch with them that very night on the battlements.

A while later, Laertes is in the midst of his preparations for his trip to France. Accompanying him is his sister, the attractive young Ophelia, to whom Hamlet has lately been making some romantic advances. Laertes warns her that she should not take the prince's attentions too seriously. Their father, old

Polonius, enters and he, too, lectures Ophelia about Hamlet, actually going so far as to forbid her to see him anymore.

Late that night, Hamlet and his companions wait, in breathless anticipation, for the Ghost to reappear. They are not disappointed. "Look, my lord, it comes!"[36] exclaims Horatio. The strange figure beckons for Hamlet to walk with it alone and, despite the other men's protests, the prince follows it to another section of the battlements. There, the Ghost reveals the awful truth that old King Hamlet did not die a natural death; he was murdered, poisoned by his brother, Claudius. "The serpent that did sting thy father's life," the Ghost tells Hamlet, "now wears his crown."[37] Horrified by this revelation, the young man learns why his father's soul has returned from purgatory—to ask his son to avenge the terrible crime perpetrated against the former king, his family, and the kingdom. But Hamlet must not harm his mother. "Leave her to heaven," the Ghost commands, "and to those thorns that in her bosom lodge / To prick and sting her."[38] At that, the apparition vanishes. Horatio and the others approach Hamlet and he makes them swear on the hilt of his sword that they will not reveal the eerie events that have just transpired.

Act Two: Has Hamlet Gone Mad?

A few days later, a much-concerned Ophelia tells her father that Hamlet recently paid her a disquieting visit. His face was pale, she tells Polonius, his clothes were a mess, he gripped her arm very hard, and then left the room without uttering a single word. Polonius decides that Hamlet's unrequited love for Ophelia has driven the young man mad, and he vows to inform the king about this disturbing development.

Several weeks go by. One day two young men, Rosencrantz and Guildenstern, friends of Prince Hamlet, arrive at Elsinore and present themselves before the king and queen, who have summoned them. Claudius and Gertrude ask the visitors to keep a close eye on Hamlet and to attempt to find out what is causing him to act so strangely. Rosencrantz and Guildenstern agree to do so.

Polonius now enters, accompanied by ambassadors from Norway, who bring the good news that war has been averted. Fortinbras has decided not to attack Denmark. Instead, he will invade Poland, and he requests that he be allowed to march his army through Denmark to reach his goal. Claudius agrees to allow the Norwegians safe passage, after which the ambassadors exit.

Next, the king and queen listen attentively to Polonius's

This nineteenth-century drawing shows Hamlet and Horatio (right) on the battlements in their eventful encounter with the Ghost.

long-winded explanation for Hamlet's recent odd behavior. They see Hamlet approaching and Polonius requests that the others leave him alone with the young man so that he can question him. Alone with Hamlet, Polonius is at first sure that the prince is indeed mad. "He is far gone, far gone!"[39] the old man says to himself. But as they continue to talk, Hamlet's ambiguous, too clever remarks make Polonius suspect that he might be only faking insanity. "Though this be madness, yet there is method in it,"[40] Polonius mutters.

After Polonius takes his leave, Rosencrantz and Guildenstern enter and greet Hamlet. He has guessed that their arrival was the work of the king and makes them admit to it. He says that they can go tell the king and queen that Hamlet's strange behavior in recent weeks is nothing of any great consequence; he is just melancholy, for some unknown reason unable to recognize and appreciate the world's many beauties and qualities. "I have of late—but wherefore [why] I know not—lost all my mirth," he complains:

This goodly frame, the earth, seems to me a sterile promontory; this most excellent canopy, the air, look you, this brave overhanging firmament [the sky], this majestical roof fretted with golden fire [the sun's rays]—why, it appeareth no other thing to me than a foul and pestilent congregation of vapors.[41]

Rosencrantz and Guildenstern proceed to tell Hamlet that a band of traveling actors is on its way to Elsinore to entertain the court, news that immediately arouses the prince's interest. The players arrive and Hamlet takes one of them aside. "Can you play *The Murder of Gonzago?*"[42] he asks the man. The actor agrees to present that play, which is about the murder of a king, before King Claudius and his court the following night and to insert a dozen or so lines composed by Hamlet himself into the text. Finally alone, the prince spills his guts. He bemoans the fact that he suspects his uncle is guilty of his father's murder and so far has been unable to prove it conclusively. But that is about to change. Hamlet will closely watch Claudius's reactions to the murder depicted in the play and see if the king responds like a guilty man. That will be the proof. Hamlet says,

I have heard

That guilty creatures, sitting at a play,

Have by the very cunning of the scene

Been struck so to the soul that presently

They have proclaimed their malefactions [crimes]. . . .

I'll observe his looks. . . .

If he but blench [flinch], I know my course. . . .

The play's the thing

Wherein I'll catch the conscience of the King![43]

Act Three: The Play Within the Play

The next day, in Elsinore's audience hall, Rosencrantz and Guildenstern tell Claudius, Gertrude, Polonius, and Ophelia that they have not been able to discover the cause of Hamlet's strange behavior. Trying to find out for themselves, Claudius and Polonius send Ophelia to a spot where she is certain to encounter Hamlet. They then hide, intending to eavesdrop on any conversation that ensues between the young man and woman.

As he approaches the spot in question, Hamlet, in one of his deeply melancholy moods, quietly wonders to himself whether life is worth living anymore. "To be, or not to be, that is the question," he says. "Whether 'tis nobler in the mind to suffer the slings and arrows of outrageous fortune or to take arms against a sea of troubles, and by opposing end them. . . . 'Tis a consummation [goal] devoutly to be wished. To die—to sleep." Still, he realizes, suicide is easier to talk about than to commit, for deep down everyone worries about what unknown terrors might be lurking in death's nether realm.

The dread of something after death—

The undiscovered country, from whose bourn no traveler returns—puzzles the will and makes us rather bear those ills we have than fly to others we know not of. Thus conscience does make cowards of us all.[44]

Hamlet's intense moment of introspection is interrupted by Ophelia's approach. Still quite angry with his mother, he is irritated by the presence of any woman, including Ophelia, about whom he once cared a great deal. He lashes out at her, saying, "Get thee to a nunnery! Why wouldst thou be a breeder of sinners? . . . I say, we will have no more marriages."[45] After he leaves, it is apparent that Ophelia is devastated. "O, woe is me to have seen what I have seen [here],"[46] she exclaims. Claudius and Polonius step forward from their hiding place and contemplate what they have heard. Claudius is sure that Hamlet is up to something that might prove dangerous to the throne; it would be best, therefore, to send him to England, where he would be safely out of the way.

A little while later, Hamlet is helping the players prepare for their performance. Taking Horatio aside, he tells him what he is up to and asks him to watch the king's reactions during the presentation. Soon, the courtroom fills with spectators and the play begins. As the action proceeds and reaches the scene in which King Gonzago is poisoned, Claudius becomes ever more restive. Finally, unable to withstand the strain any longer, he breaks, screaming, "Give me some light! Away!"[47] A commotion ensues and the hall quickly empties, leaving Hamlet and Horatio alone. This is Hamlet's moment of triumph. He has his proof that his uncle is indeed guilty of foul murder.

At that moment, Rosencrantz and Guildenstern arrive and inform the prince that his mother, who is upset about his recent behavior, has summoned him to her bedchamber for a talk. Having heard that Hamlet will be meeting his mother, Polonius

Hamlet (sitting at left) closely watches the reactions of Claudius (wearing crown in right foreground), as the players enact The Murder of Gonzago.

Confronting his mother, the frustrated Hamlet demands to know how she could have married Claudius, a man so clearly inferior to her former husband.

tells Claudius that he plans to hide in the queen's chamber and afterward report everything he has heard to the king.

On the way to the meeting, Hamlet notices Claudius praying at a small altar. "O, my offense is rank," the king declares emotionally, "it smells to heaven; it hath the primal eldest curse upon it, a brother's murder [a reference to Cain's slaying of his brother Abel in the Bible]!"[48] While Claudius prays for forgiveness, Hamlet steals up behind him and raises his sword to strike. But at the last instant he hesitates, fearing that a man killed during prayer might receive God's blessing and thereby escape eternal damnation.

Hamlet continues on toward his mother's chamber, where Gertrude watches Polonius hide himself behind a wall-hanging. Entering, the prince angrily accuses the queen of being unfaithful to her former husband. Soon, Polonius makes a noise, and Hamlet, assuming that it is Claudius hiding behind the drapery, jumps forward, draws his sword, and stabs straight through. However the young man is disappointed to discover that it is only the meddlesome lord chamberlain that he has killed. Hamlet now returns to berating his mother for her infidelity; but his father's ghost appears (unseen by Gertrude) and reminds him of his promise not to harm his mother. Calming down, the prince takes his leave, dragging Polonius's body along with him.

Act Four: Hamlet Marked for Death

Gertrude informs Claudius that Hamlet had slain Polonius. At first, the prince refuses to tell where he has hidden the body, but eventually he admits that it lies rotting beneath the stairs of the castle's lobby. Claudius realizes that the time for sending Hamlet away is past due and orders him to embark for England, accompanied by Rosencrantz and Guildenstern. Unbeknownst to the prince, the king gives the two courtiers letters to be given to the authorities in England. The letters instruct that, by royal order, Hamlet is to be killed immediately on his arrival there.

Sometime after Hamlet's departure, Gertrude, Claudius, and Horatio witness a pitiful, heartrending scene. Ophelia, having lost touch with reality, wanders about aimlessly, singing and muttering to herself. It is apparent that her loss of Hamlet's love, coupled with her father's recent grisly death, has driven her over the edge and into madness. As she leaves, her brother Laertes suddenly arrives, accompanied by some armed men. He had heard about his father's death and assumed that Claudius was the murderer. "Let come what comes," the young man cries out, "only I'll be revenged most thoroughly for my father!"[49] Claudius and Gertrude insist that the king did not kill Polonius. Just then, Ophelia reappears and her horrified brother sees that she has slipped into mental oblivion. Claudius promises Laertes that he will do what he can to help him achieve his revenge, both for his father's death and his sister's undoing.

Not long afterward, a sailor gives Horatio a letter from Hamlet. According to the letter, while on his way to England the prince was captured by pirates, who are now holding him for ransom. As Horatio hurries off to help obtain his friend's release, a messenger delivers another letter from Hamlet, this one addressed to the king himself. The note informs Claudius that the prince will not be going to England after all, but instead will be returning to Elsinore in the near future. The king has already told Laertes that Hamlet is the one who murdered Polonius. Claudius and Laertes now hatch a sinister plot designed to rid themselves and the world of the troublesome prince of Denmark. When Hamlet comes home, the king will arrange a "friendly" fencing match between Hamlet and Laertes; but the match will be rigged in Laertes'

Ophelia twirls aimlessly in her mad scene. Never a strong person, she has snapped under the pressure of emotional strain.

favor, for the tip of his sword will be coated with poison, which will kill Hamlet when it grazes his skin. "I bought an unction [oil] of a mountebank [a seller of quack cures]," Laertes says, "so mortal [deadly] that, but dip a knife in it . . . [and nothing] can save the thing from death that is but scratched."[50] In case this plan should fail, Claudius will also prepare a poisoned drink to offer to Hamlet.

Suddenly, the queen enters bearing sad news. Ophelia, her mind no longer sound, has accidentally drowned herself. She "fell in the weeping brook," Gertrude explains.

Her clothes spread wide

And, mermaid-like, awhile they bore her up

. . . but long it could not be

49

Till that her garments, heavy with their drink,

Pulled the poor wretch from her melodious lay [song]

To muddy death.[51]

Blaming Hamlet for his sister's demise, Laertes now has double the reason for wanting to see the prince die.

Act Five: The Hall Littered with Bodies

The scene shifts to a churchyard near the castle, a few days later. Two gravediggers are excavating a pit for a coffin. As they debate whether the young woman who will be buried there died of natural causes or suicide, Hamlet and Horatio appear. The prince falls into a conversation with one of the gravediggers, who finds some old skulls and tosses them out of the hole as he works. "How long hast thou been a grave-maker?" Hamlet inquires.

The "poor wretch" Ophelia, with her "garments heavy with their drink," floats to her doom in this shot from Olivier's film.

GRAVEDIGGER: Of all the days of i' the year, I came to't that day

That our last king Hamlet overcame [old] Fortinbras.

HAMLET: How long is that since?

GRAVEDIGGER: It was that very day that young Hamlet was born—he that is mad, and sent into England.

HAMLET: Why was he sent into England?

GRAVEDIGGER: Why, because he was mad. . . .

HAMLET: How long will a man lie i' the earth ere [before] he rot?

GRAVEDIGGER: Faith, if he be not rotten before he die . . . he will last you some eight year or nine year.[52]

The gravedigger then throws out another skull and identifies it as belonging to one Yorick, a former royal jester. Taking the relic and holding it gently, Hamlet muses on the inevitability of death for all people, remembering fondly:

Alas, poor Yorick! I knew him, Horatio. A fellow of infinite jest, of most excellent fancy. He hath borne me on his back a thousand times. . . . Where be your jibes now? . . . your songs . . . your flashes of merriment that were wont to set the table on a roar? Not one now, to mock your own grinning?[53]

Suddenly, a funeral procession approaches and Hamlet and Horatio step back to watch. As the mourners gather around the grave, Laertes, overcome with grief, jumps in to hold his sister's body one last time. Seeing this, Hamlet realizes who is being buried and he too leaps into the hole, where the two men begin fighting. Luckily, some of the attendants manage to separate the men.

Hamlet (with arms outstretched in foreground) rushes forward in anguish to embrace the dead Ophelia.

Later, back in the castle, Hamlet stands talking to Horatio. The prince tells his friend how he had earlier managed to foil the plot involving the letters given by Claudius to Rosencrantz and Guildenstern. While on his way to England, Hamlet had discovered the deadly contents of the letters and managed to rewrite them. When the two courtiers escaped the pirates and made their way to England, it was they, rather than Hamlet, who were immediately executed by the authorities.

At that moment, one of Claudius's courtiers, Osric, appears and informs Hamlet that the king has set up a fencing match between the prince and Laertes. Despite Horatio's warning not to attend, Hamlet tells Osric that he accepts and will be there shortly. The entire court assembles to watch the contest, which begins in a seemingly friendly manner. Hamlet scores first, after which Claudius offers him the cup of poisoned wine. But the prince refuses, saying that he would rather fight a while longer before he drinks. Hamlet scores again. This time, Queen Gertrude, desiring to toast her son's win, drinks a goblet of wine. His eyes widening in horror, Claudius realizes too late that it is the one bearing the poison. As the fight continues, Laertes manages to wound Hamlet, who, suddenly angered that his opponent has drawn blood, begins to fight in earnest. In the scuffle, the men drop their swords, unknowingly exchange them, and Hamlet wounds Laertes with the poisoned blade. Then the queen falls from her chair, causing a shocked gasp to ripple through the audience. "O my dear Hamlet!" she cries. "The drink, the drink! I am poisoned!"[54] Seconds later, she is dead.

At this, the stout Laertes, himself now dying from the effects of poison, admits aloud his and the king's treachery. "Hamlet, thou art slain; / No medicine in the world can do thee good. . . . / The treacherous instrument is in thy hand. . . . / The king, the king's to blame."[55] As all eyes fall on Claudius, Hamlet leaps at the frightened man and plunges the poisoned blade repeatedly into his body, then forces him to drink from the poisoned goblet. Claudius collapses in a heap and promptly dies. Then Laertes, his voice becoming weak, begs Hamlet's forgiveness; but before the prince is able to give it, the fog of death clouds young Laertes' eyes.

A few minutes later, shots are heard in the distance and Osric announces that Fortinbras, back from Poland, is approaching with his troops to pay his respects. By now, the poison is taking its toll on Hamlet, whom Horatio holds in his arms. "O, I die, Horatio!" the stricken prince gasps. "The potent poison quite o'ercrows my spirit." After announcing his friendship and support for Fortinbras, Hamlet is able to say only four more words: "The rest is silence."[56] A quiet moment follows. Then Horatio speaks. "Now cracks a noble heart," he whispers, his voice choked with emotion. "Good night, sweet prince, and flights of angels sing thee to thy rest!"[57]

Fortinbras makes his stately entrance only to find, to his surprise and dismay, that the hall is littered with bodies. He orders four captains to form an honor guard and bear Hamlet "like a soldier to the stage." Had he lived, says Fortinbras, he would have made a fine ruler, and the least he deserves is a volley of shots fired to commemorate his untimely passing. As the men carry away the young prince's body in a solemn death march, Fortinbras orders, "Go, bid the soldiers shoot."[58]

In a solemn death march, four captains bear Hamlet's body away. Had he lived, Fortinbras remarks, he would have been a worthy ruler.

CHAPTER FOUR

The Principal Characters Appearing in *Hamlet*

The characters in Shakespeare's *Hamlet* can be conveniently divided into general groups; all, that is, except for Hamlet himself, who stands by himself, the lonely, troubled figure around which the play's action swirls. He interacts with the other characters, sometimes singly and other times in their various groups, as need dictates.

Of these character groups, the most prominent and pivotal is what might be termed the royal triangle. It is composed of the present king, Claudius (Hamlet's uncle); his wife, Gertrude (Hamlet's mother); and the Ghost of old King Hamlet (Hamlet's father). The very existence of this triangle, highlighted by the questionable marriage of Claudius and Gertrude, is what upsets Hamlet and drives most of his actions.

Another crucial group of characters consists of the royal chamberlain, Polonius, and his children, Laertes and Ophelia.

All three are at odds with Hamlet throughout most of the story. Hamlet's friends—Horatio, Rosencrantz, and Guildenstern—making up a third character group, have small but important roles that help to move the plot along. Minor character groups supporting the major groups include courtiers attending Denmark's rulers; commoners, among them soldiers, gravediggers, actors, and messengers; and foreigners, including ambassadors from Norway and England, and Fortinbras, a Norwegian prince.

This sounds like a great many characters, requiring many actors. Today, in films and occasional very large stage productions of *Hamlet*, each role is usually played by a separate actor. However, in Shakespeare's time the practice of "character doubling"—one actor playing two or more roles—was widespread, and this practice is still frequently employed, especially by small acting troupes attempting to keep down production costs. It was and is fairly common, therefore, for an actor playing a small role, such as the soldier Marcellus, who appears at the beginning of the play, to show up later as one or more messengers or courtiers. This reality of Shakespearean production should be kept in mind while examining the following list of the play's principal characters. (For the sake of convenience, they are listed in alphabetical order, rather than by their importance.)

Bernardo and Marcellus

The first characters the audience sees when the curtain rises, they are guards on the night watch on Elsinore's battlements. On the two previous nights they have seen a ghost there and when Hamlet's friend Horatio joins them they tell him about it. With him, they witness still another visit by the apparition, and later they accompany him when he informs Hamlet about it.

Though Bernardo and Marcellus are minor characters, they carry an important responsibility. Aided by appropriate sets and lighting effects, they must help to establish the atmospheric, supernatural tone of the crucial opening scene. And they have to make the audience believe that they are common, everyday people who have been thrust into an extraordinary situation. On the one hand, they must react to the Ghost with a credible amount of awe and fear. But they must not appear to be too overwhelmed by these feelings, or else the audience will get the impression that Denmark's soldiers are not tough and brave enough to defend the castle and the realm.

Occasionally, a minor Shakespearean character has a line that over the years has become very famous. Indeed, one spoken by Marcellus is perhaps second only to Hamlet's "To be or not to be" in the play's long list of recognizable phrases. Just after Hamlet and the Ghost walk off to talk alone, Marcellus mutters, "Something is rotten in the state of Denmark."[59]

Claudius, King of Denmark

Brother to old King Hamlet and uncle to young Prince Hamlet, Claudius is the villain of the piece. An ambitious man, he murders his brother and soon afterward marries his sister-in-law, Gertrude (before the play begins). At first, Claudius attempts to get along with the prince. But as time goes on, Hamlet begins to appear dangerous to the new royal regime. The turning point is when the players enact *The Murder of Gonzago* before Claudius and the play's staged murder reminds him of his recent crime against the former king. Realizing that the prince must be eliminated, Claudius sends letters ordering Hamlet's execution to the English authorities. When this plan fails, the king hatches a more desperate scheme, this time with Laertes. The two arrange for Laertes to duel with Hamlet and stick him with a sword bearing a potent poison, but this plan also backfires. The deadly sword ends up killing Claudius (as well as Hamlet and Laertes).

Although many of his deeds are clearly evil, Claudius is no ordinary villain, especially by Shakespearean standards. First, he seems to be an able administrator. Once he has managed to usurp the Danish throne, he appears to be intent on being an effective, even-handed ruler. In fact, Michael Pennington suggests,

> His usurpation could have been a blessing for Denmark, if it hadn't been for Hamlet [and his quest to punish his father's killer]. The old king's regime [based on what we hear characters say about it] seems bleak, unprofessional, too full of unregulated loyalties and unreliable transactions.[60]

Also, and very importantly, Claudius feels guilty about his crime. In the third scene of the third act he has a long, powerful speech in which he admits his motives for killing his brother: "My crown, mine own ambition, and my queen."[61] Yet at the same time, he is attempting to pray for forgiveness, searching for

Claudius (foreground) senses that all is not well with his stepson, Hamlet (right), who still mourns his father, Old Hamlet.

some way to make restitution for his offense. "This whole complex, tortuous speech is remarkable for a villain," says noted Shakespearean scholar Peter Quennell. "It is the kind of agonized struggle with conscience that is more usually associated with tragic heroes (e.g., Macbeth). Claudius is Shakespeare's most complex, and subtly rendered, villain."[62]

Eventually, of course, Claudius must pay the ultimate price for his misdeeds. But it is a tribute to Shakespeare's skill at characterization that when Hamlet triumphs in the end, it is not over a mere cardboard villain but rather an opponent of considerable depth and talent. That triumph is therefore more remarkable and admirable.

Fortinbras, Prince of Norway

He has few lines and little time onstage. He appears only briefly in the fourth scene of the fourth act as he leads his soldiers through Denmark on the way to attack Poland. He is not even mentioned again until he arrives in the finale to find all the members of the Danish royal family dead. Hearing that, before dying, Hamlet gave him his blessings and support, Fortinbras says that he will take charge of Denmark's throne. To strengthen his legitimacy, he makes a vague reference to some legal claims: "I have some rights of memory in this kingdom, / Which now to claim my vantage doth invite me."[63] Then the Norwegian prince honors Hamlet by having his body borne away with full military honors.

Although his stage time is limited, Fortinbras is a character of considerable significance. First, early on he poses a very real threat to the stability of Claudius's regime; only by some clever diplomacy is Hamlet's uncle able to avert war and keep Denmark intact and prosperous. Here, as well as at the play's end, Fortinbras adds a political dimension to the action, reminding the audience that larger forces are at work beyond the narrower boundaries of Hamlet's obsessed efforts to achieve personal revenge.

Also, Shakespeare fashioned the character of Fortinbras to parallel, and thereby to highlight, that of Hamlet. Like Denmark's prince, Fortinbras is the son of a deceased king whose brother is now on the throne. Also like Hamlet, the Norwegian prince is out to avenge an injury done to his father (in this case, the loss of lands to old King Hamlet in a prior war).

Gertrude, Queen of Denmark

Hamlet's mother is unaware that her brother-in-law, Claudius, murdered her former husband. In the interest of keeping the realm stable and strong at a time when Norway is threatening to invade, she marries Claudius (shortly before the play begins). She also apparently admires him and is sexually attracted to him (although she and Claudius are never intimate in any way during the course of the action). Gertrude seems consistently sincere and desirous that there be harmony in the royal court, as well as between her son and new husband. She is genuinely concerned about Hamlet's moodiness and melancholy, and she is befuddled and frightened when he verbally attacks her in her bedchamber in the fourth scene of the third act. Finally, she displays true courage, nobility, and self-sacrifice when, during the climactic sword fight, she drinks from the poisoned goblet, revealing Claudius's treachery.

Thousands of pages have been written attempting to analyze Gertrude's character and find out what motivates her actions. This is far from easy. Throughout the play, she appears rather formal and dutiful, if not submissive, to her new husband, and she almost never mentions aloud her true feelings about anyone or anything. This leaves her role, one quite central to the plot, particularly open to interpretation by actresses, directors, and scholars alike.

As a result, this queen has come to be depicted in ways that the author may not have originally intended. The most common modern approach is to play her, in the words of University of Northern Texas scholar Rebecca Smith, as "a vain, self-satisfied woman of strong physical and sexual appetites." In the 1969 film of the play, Smith points out, the director "repeatedly shows her eating and drinking" and "greedily swilling wine." And in Laurence Olivier's famous 1948 film,

> Her relationship with her son is tinged with sexuality. Olivier's Hamlet brutally hurls Gertrude—the ultimate sexual object—onto her bed, alternating embraces and abuse. . . . The misrepresentations that these film versions of Gertrude perpetuate . . . seem to assume that only a deceitful, highly sexual woman could arouse such strong responses and violent reactions in men.[64]

By contrast, strictly on paper Shakespeare's Gertrude is a much more sympathetic character. First, there is no doubt that he intended her to be innocent of any knowledge of or complicity in the death of old King Hamlet. In this regard it is revealing to compare his version of her with that in earlier versions of the story. In the original Danish version, the character knowingly marries her husband's killer, and in Belleforest's sixteenth-century version, she is said to have committed adultery with her brother-in-law while still married to her first husband. Shakespeare eliminated these elements and made his Gertrude more of an innocent sex object manipulated by her husband and son and frustrated by her desire to love and please both of them.[65]

Ghost of Hamlet's Father

This apparition appears on the castle's battlements and provides the crucial piece of information that drives much of the play's plot—namely that Claudius murdered his own brother, old King Hamlet. "Sleeping within my orchard," the Ghost recalls,

My custom always of the afternoon,

Upon my secure hour thy uncle stole,

With juice of cursed hebenon [poison] in a vial,

And in the porches of my ears did pour

The leperous distilment. . . .

Thus was I, sleeping, by my brother's hand

Of life, of crown, of queen, at once dispatched [deprived of by dying].[66]

The Ghost then calls on Hamlet to seek revenge for this foul deed. Later, in the fourth scene of the third act, when Hamlet is berating his mother, the ghastly visitor reappears and warns him to ease up on her.

Clearly, the creature that haunts Elsinore is not friendly. The spirit of old King Hamlet is meant to be a scary character, as evidenced by the frightened reactions of Marcellus, Bernardo, and Horatio. In fact, even though it became a ghost through foul play and no fault of its own, it seems more evil than good. As Horatio points out, "it started [jumped] like a guilty thing"[67] at the sudden crowing of the cock, signaling the coming of morning and pure sunlight. There is no indication in the lines of why the Ghost should be so dark and frightening. Perhaps in death old Hamlet is paying a heavy price for some of his own sins committed in life.

On the other hand, the Ghost may appear as it does because it is an instrument of divine or supernatural wrath and justice. As Philip Edwards, of the University of Liverpool, points out,

> The Ghost's commands [for Hamlet to punish Claudius and to allow heaven to deal with Gertrude] indicate not the pursuit of personal satisfaction but the existence of a world beyond the human world responsible for justice in the human world. . . . [And therefore] the play of *Hamlet* takes place within the possibility that there is a higher court of values than those which operate around us.[68]

Gravediggers

In the original Shakespearean texts, these two characters were referred to as "clowns," but eventually they became known as gravediggers, which more accurately describes them, since digging graves is what they do for a living. Shakespeare may have called them clowns because they provide comic relief in a story that is otherwise very serious and gloomy. Indeed, the principal gravedigger is a lighthearted fellow—a "saloon-bar philosopher"[69] according to Michael Pennington—whose wit matches that of the title character himself. When Hamlet asks him whose grave he is digging, he replies, "Mine, sir."

> HAMLET: I think it be thine indeed, for thou liest in it.
>
> GRAVEDIGGER: You lie out on't [outside of it], sir, and therefore 'tis not yours.
>
> For my part, I do not lie in't, yet it is mine.
>
> HAMLET: Thou dost lie in't, to be in't and say it is thine.
>
> 'Tis for the dead, not for the quick; therefore thou liest.
>
> GRAVEDIGGER: 'Tis a quick lie, sir; 'twill away again from me to you.[70]

As anyone who has seen a production of the play knows, the chief gravedigger is a small but excellent part that often attracts the best comic actors. (Billy Crystal played the part in Kenneth Branagh's 1997 film.) On stage, the actor playing this role often doubles as the Ghost or leader of the Players.

Hamlet, Prince of Denmark

Unlike Gertrude, Hamlet quite often expresses his personal feelings about people and things. He clearly reveres his father's memory, hates his uncle, and finds his mother's recent actions inexplicable and frustrating, and he frequently vents his feelings and emotions in some of the most splendid lines and speeches ever written. As shown through both his words and actions, Hamlet is also perceptive, witty, worldly, crafty, and poetic. These attributes of the character regularly attract the greatest (along with some of the not so great) actors of each succeeding generation.

But what actors, as well as audiences and scholars, find even more fascinating about Hamlet is what he does *not* say and do, for his character is often flawed, ambiguous, and hard to understand. It is never quite clear, for instance, whether Hamlet's insanity is a complete fabrication, as it appears to be on the surface. The rapid succession of shocks he has endured—his father's death, his mother's sudden remarriage, and the discovery that his uncle murdered his father—might well have combined to make him temporarily or even permanently irrational. Even more inscrutable is his constant indecision and failure to act (as when, for example, he hesitates and shrinks away from killing Claudius while the man is praying). The narrator of Olivier's great film calls him a man "who could not make up his mind," and there is a fair amount of truth in this statement.

Not surprisingly, then, actors of all conceivable backgrounds, mannerisms, physical and vocal gifts, and so forth, have attempted to find the "core" or "center" of the character. In the process, they have generated a wide range of quite distinctive interpretations. The great John Gielgud, for instance, felt that, despite the character's relentless preoccupation with getting revenge, violence is not in his nature. Gielgud saw and played Hamlet as a gentle man trapped in circumstances beyond his control and therefore forced, against his will and better judgment, to enact revenge. In this and other similar interpretations, the character has no close friends, no one to confide in or guide him. He makes up his mind about what to do by talking to himself (in soliloquies, speeches recited when alone). As it happens, the decisions he makes unfortunately lead to many deaths, including his own.

By contrast, the controversial Hamlet of Olivier's film is harried and coerced by external rather than internal forces, especially dark and bizarre ones. In approaching the role, Olivier was influenced by the ideas of two famous early-twentieth-century psychoanalysts, Sigmund Freud and Ernest Jones. They concluded that Hamlet suffers from an Oedipus complex, a repressed hatred for his dead father and sexual desire for his mother. In this view, Hamlet delays killing Claudius, and thereby fulfilling his revenge, because subconsciously he wants the same thing Claudius does, namely Gertrude. On some level the young man realizes that he is no better than his uncle, and that if he kills Claudius he must also rid the world of himself. In his film, Olivier emphasized Hamlet's repressed feelings for the queen by increasing the duration of the kisses between mother and son and having the camera linger suggestively on Gertrude's bed.

Hamlet and Gertrude argue over her marriage to Claudius. Olivier injected a touch of the Freudian "Oedipus complex" in his portrayal.

Another controversial Hamlet, played by David Warner in Britain's 1966 Royal Shakespeare Company production, took a completely different approach. Following director Peter Hall's concept, Warner played the prince as a young, idealistic nonconformist, a rebel very much like the "new left," anti-establishment youth that came to be identified with the 1960s. The hippies and other new left radicals were impatient with their elders and disillusioned by rampant political and social corruption. Warner's Hamlet is similarly disillusioned by the corrupt establishment at Elsinore, which can be "cleansed" only by the prince's honesty and righteous sense of outrage, but alas, he finds himself unable to act. As Hall puts it, Hamlet's disillusionment

> produces an apathy of the will so deep that commitment to politics, to religion or to life is impossible. For a man said to do nothing, Hamlet does a great deal. . . . He is always on the brink of action, but something inside him, this disease of disillusionment, stops the final, committed action.[71]

What makes the character and the play so great is that all of these interpretations, and perhaps countless others, are equally valid.

Horatio

A school friend of Hamlet's who is visiting Elsinore, Horatio, along with Marcellus and Bernardo, observes the Ghost, informs Hamlet about the experience, and sticks around as Hamlet's close confidant throughout the rest of the play. There is no doubt that the prince feels he can trust Horatio; otherwise he would not confide in him his plans for proving the king's guilt by staging *The Murder of Gonzago*. Indeed, in the second scene of the third act, Hamlet praises his friend, saying, "Give me that man / That is not passion's slave, and I will wear him / In my heart's core, ay, in my heart of hearts, / As I do thee."[72]

As acting parts go, that of Horatio is not particularly rewarding. He has little depth and mostly just follows Hamlet around and observes the action. One saving grace for the actor cast in the role is that he has the good fortune to recite one of the most beautiful and emotional lines in all of English literature: "Now cracks a noble heart. Good night, sweet prince, / And flights of angels sing thee to thy rest!"[73]

Laertes

Polonius's son and Ophelia's brother, Laertes warns his sister not to waste her time with Hamlet, who, he suggests, will only end up discarding her. Laertes then leaves for France, where a man sent by his father spies on him. Later, hearing of Polonius's death, the young man rushes home and becomes a willing participant in Claudius's schemes to kill Hamlet. Finally, Laertes fights in the climactic duel in which both young men are killed.

As he did with Fortinbras, Shakespeare used Laertes to parallel Hamlet's character and situation. Like the other two headstrong young men, Laertes is intent on achieving retribution for wrongs done to his father (in this case Polonius's death at Hamlet's hands). Hamlet himself acknowledges the similarity of their situations when he says, "By the image of my cause I see / The portraiture of his."[74] However, Laertes and Hamlet are very different as characters. Though earnest, Laertes is rather insensitive, humorless, and boorish, and actors playing him often try to make up for these negative traits by emphasizing (and sometimes overdoing) his seeming change of heart in his death scene.

Ophelia

She is Polonius's daughter and Laertes' sister. She is also Hamlet's "love interest," although audiences only *hear* about their courtship, which takes place before the play begins. Polonius mentions it in the third scene of the first act, as does

Ophelia, who says that Hamlet has "of late made many ten-ders / Of his affection to me."[75]

In the course of the play, though, Ophelia experiences only abuse and tragedy. First, her brother and father rather curtly dismiss her very real love for Hamlet. Then the prince, caught up in his own obsessions and frustrations, insults and rejects her. Finally, she hears that her former boyfriend, whom she believes has gone mad, has murdered her father. All this is too much for her innocent, frail personality and she goes off the deep end (literally as well as figuratively, since she ends up drowning in a stream).

Ophelia's death has long been a favorite subject of painters. Perhaps the most famous example is Englishman John Everett Millais's 1852 masterpiece showing her floating down the stream face up with one hand raised limply above the water's surface. Director Laurence Olivier consciously tried to reproduce the look of this image in Ophelia's death scene in his famous film of *Hamlet*.

A view of John Everett Millais's famous painting of Ophelia floating to her death. (Compare to the image from Olivier's film on page 50.)

Polonius

The lord high chamberlain of the Danish royal court and father to Ophelia and Laertes, Polonius is a long-winded know-it-all, a busybody, and a classic court schemer. After forbidding his daughter to see any more of Hamlet, he becomes obsessed with the idea that the royal prince is madly in love with Ophelia and that he has gone mad because he cannot have her. This is the motivation for several scenes in which the conniving old man eavesdrops on Hamlet's conversations. The last instance, in which he hides in Gertrude's bedchamber, proves his undoing, for Hamlet detects his presence and stabs him to death.

Polonius, is a schemer and manipulator who shows no particular affection for his children, Laertes and Ophelia.

In addition to being a deceitful and dangerous schemer, Polonius is a lousy parent. He pays no attention to his daughter's assertion that she loves Hamlet and nowhere in the play does the old man utter a single word of affection for either of his children. Furthermore, he readily spies on both of them to advance his own or the king's aims.

Still, Polonius possesses one quality that redeems him somewhat in the eyes of audiences and makes his role attractive to character actors. "Shakespeare being Shakespeare," Pennington explains,

> having created this unsavory man, he then makes him enjoyable company in the theater. . . . Polonius is made palatable by the fact that he is funny. . . . He rouses Hamlet to some fine improvisations, and his

garrulousness [talkative nature] and pedantry [obsession with rules] are turned into more or less innocent comedy. So the part has to be played by an actor who is a merciless character man but also has the gifts of a stand-up comedian.[76]

Rosencrantz and Guildenstern

These Danish courtiers always appear together and seem inseparable. Yet they never discuss anything with each other and seem content simply to address other characters and react to what is happening around them. Supposedly they are student friends of Hamlet, like Horatio. But the events of the play do not demonstrate much that can be called friendship. Claudius asks them secretly to find out why Hamlet is behaving so strangely. Later, the king orders them to accompany the prince to England and gives them sealed orders for the prince's death. Hamlet discovers the plan, replaces his name with theirs, and they end up dying in England.

Though minor characters in *Hamlet*, Rosencrantz and Guildenstern have the leading roles in playwright Tom Stoppard's 1967 play, *Rosencrantz and Guildenstern Are Dead*. In a brilliant stroke, Stoppard cleverly interwove lines from Shakespeare's play with new dialogue. Hamlet is one of the minor characters, and lines and situations treated seriously by Shakespeare become absurd and humorous in this new context. At one point, for instance, Guildenstern loses his temper and stabs one of the actors who is visiting Elsinore, an incident that would seem to mirror the many violent deaths in *Hamlet*. But then the "dead" man gets up, unhurt; unbeknownst to Guildenstern, the dagger he used is a harmless stage prop. Somewhere, surely, Shakespeare is smiling.

CHAPTER FIVE

Exploring the Basic Truths of the Human Experience

In addition to its tens of thousands of stage presentations over the years, *Hamlet* has been filmed nearly fifty times, with stars ranging from Sir Laurence Olivier to Mel Gibson in the title role. A testimonial to the play's universality is that a number of these movies were made in Italy, India, the African nation of Ghana, and other foreign cultures seemingly far removed from the story's original setting of medieval Denmark. *Hamlet* has also inspired some twenty-six ballets, six operas, and dozens of other musical works. It is the most often quoted, written about, and studied play in the world, with hundreds of new books, articles, and reviews appearing every year.

What makes *Hamlet* so appealing to so many people in so many different cultures, artistic media, professions, and walks of life? In part, it is that the play develops and examines certain themes and ideas with which a majority of people readily identify.

In exploring some of the basic truths of the human experience and condition, *Hamlet* regularly reaches out to, touches, and affects people. Through the play's characters and actions, Phyllis Abrahms and Alan Brody point out, "Shakespeare probes the nature of death, of fate, of madness. He reveals the eternal conflicts between reality and illusion, faith and despair, the mind and the body."[77] Because each succeeding generation contemplates anew these essential human themes and values, each invariably searches *Hamlet* for some fresh insight or new twist on an old idea. For these reasons, the play will no doubt remain in future ages just as much an endless source of theatrical and literary fascination as it is today. As noted drama professor Marvin Rosenberg puts it,

> We will all keep on learning new things about *Hamlet* as long as people love poetry and drama. Like the actors who wish they could play it forever, I could go on reading and writing about the play at least as long, and learn new things every day. Again—*Hamlet* is bottomless.[78]

A Man Tortured by Indecision

One of the most-often cited themes of the play is the title character's tendency to delay, to put off getting his revenge; some have gone so far as to call it an inability to act. Indeed, onto the tired formula of the revenge play Shakespeare superimposed a gripping psychological drama about a man tortured by indecision. Should Hamlet take the "natural" but "uncivilized" action of enacting his revenge? Or should he find some other, less violent, and therefore more civilized way of dealing with his grief and anger? We get the impression that he feels he will eventually resort to violence. But how should Claudius die? And where and when? How long will Hamlet wait before he acts?

People everywhere can relate to such feelings of conflict and irresolution. At some point, almost everyone has faced making a choice, knowing that whichever option is selected will forever alter his or her life. And those at such critical junctures have often found themselves, at least momentarily, paralyzed by indecision. This is especially true when one is choosing between violent and nonviolent means to solve a problem. Surely this is a factor that makes the character and the play so universally appealing and fascinating. As Michael Pennington astutely observes,

> One of the reasons audiences admire the play so much is that everybody in their own lives . . . faces the kind of crisis that Hamlet faces, that is, do you behave like a reactive [emotion-driven] savage or like a rational and sensitive human being?[79]

To the question of exactly why Hamlet delays so long, there is no easy answer. Among the many theories and explanations, this one, by literary critic Michael Goldman, is logical and believable:

> The question to be asked here is not why does Hamlet delay, but why does the play delay—why are *we* delayed? There is more than a grain of truth in the . . . statement that Hamlet delays because there would be no play if he did not. . . . As soon as Hamlet enters [the room where the king, Claudius, is praying] we know he will not kill the king. He cannot kill Claudius at prayer, not for theological reasons, sound as they may be, but [because] it is undramatic, too easy. The king's back is to him. There is no source of resistance. The play is going elsewhere. The action, we realize, would not satisfy us, though, like Hamlet, we have longed for it since the first act. If Shakespeare ever played with an audience, it is here. Once again, our desire for significant action is drawn upon in a way that also arouses our latent sense of how difficult this appetite is to satisfy.[80]

Despair, Disillusionment, and Loneliness

Another emotion that people everywhere can readily understand and relate to is despair. It is best described as feelings of frustration and hopelessness so intense that one wants to scream out loud, break something, strike out at someone, or, in the most extreme cases, do away with oneself. The theme of despair twists like an expanding root system through *Hamlet,* penetrating and enveloping several of the characters. There is, for example, the Ghost's despair that it has been deeply wronged and sent into death's bleak realm well before its time; and Ophelia's despair on losing first Hamlet and then her father is so strong that she goes mad.

It is Hamlet's despair, however, that the play explores most fully. He expresses it repeatedly, some of the more familiar examples being "O that this too too solid flesh would melt, / Thaw, and resolve itself into a dew! / Or that the Everlasting [God] had not fixed / His cannon against [i.e., condemned] self-slaughter!"[81]; "I have of late . . . lost all my mirth"[82]; "To be or not to be, that is the question"[83]; and "Go to, I'll no more on't! it hath made me mad!"[84] Clearly, his feelings of frustration, anger, and helplessness stem partly from his bitterness about the unhappy turns his life has taken. His father has been murdered; the killer has usurped the throne, depriving the prince of his rightful inheritance; and the queen has married the very same villain. Surely, anyone who found himself in Hamlet's place would be overcome with some of the same negative feelings he expresses.

In fact, Hamlet's despair is so intense that he is becoming disillusioned with the world and life itself, a sad and unhealthy situation for a person so young and vital. In the second scene of the second act, he tells Rosencrantz and Guildenstern, "It goes so heavily with my disposition [nature, feelings], that this goodly frame, the earth, seems to me a sterile promontory [bleak landscape]." The air and the sky should fill him with wonder and joy. But instead, they appear to him "a foul and pestilent congregation of vapors." He follows these remarks with a brief, magnificently worded query about human nature and worth that, in varying forms, has been asked again and again throughout the ages. He says in essence that people are often told that a human being is a wonderful and special creation, but what if in reality, humans were nothing but spiritless matter and their lives ultimately meaningless?

> What a piece of work is a man! how noble in reason! how infinite in faculties! in form and moving how express and admirable! in action how like an angel! in apprehension how like a god! the beauty of the world, the paragon [most perfect example] of animals! And yet to me what is this quintessence [purest essence] of dust?[85]

This speech illustrates part of why Hamlet is a character for all times, places, and peoples: He asks some of the more profound and soul-searching questions that have always intrigued and will no doubt always continue to haunt the human race.

Hamlet's despair also stems from his loneliness, still another feeling to which many people can relate. "Now I am alone,"[86] he says shortly after addressing the actors visiting Elsinore; it can be argued that he means more by this than simply that everyone else has left the room. Part of Hamlet's loneliness is the result of the situation in which he finds himself. His father, whom he idolized, has been snatched away from him; he feels alienated by his mother and uncle; and his relationship with his girlfriend is falling apart. Yet much of the prince's loneliness comes from within himself. He is a decidedly self-centered and self-absorbed individual who trusts no one (except perhaps Horatio). As scholar Salvador de Madariaga points out, it is no wonder that he talks to himself so much:

> This is the inevitable outcome of self-centeredness. Just as he forces every character and every action to

enter the stage of his soul . . . so he drives all the dialogues within his own thought, turning them into monologues [his many soliloquies]. . . . By dint of abolishing every human being but himself, he can talk to no one but himself. . . . Here lies the tragedy. The self-centered man gives nothing to the human beings that surround him; he wipes them out of existence so far as he is concerned—but he needs them. . . . For, by nature, the self-centered man is lonely—inwardly lonely, and, unless he can drown this inner loneliness in outer company, he is bound to fall into . . . melancholy and even madness.[87]

A Corrupted World

Hamlet's loneliness is, of course, an internal condition. By contrast, another theme *Hamlet* explores—corruption—is more external in nature. In the play, Shakespeare paints a vivid picture of a royal court, a kingdom, and indeed a whole world infected and tainted by dishonesty, betrayal, scheming, spying, abuse, murder, aggression, and war. In page after page, speech after speech, he leads us inexorably to an inevitable conclusion—that such behaviors will ultimately consume and destroy all that employ them.

In one of the most famous modern studies of this play, the noted Shakespearean critic Rebecca West examines Hamlet's corrupted world and concludes that he is "disgusted by his own kind."[88] As an example, she draws an unsavory (though not totally unsympathetic) portrait of Ophelia. West contends that the young woman is a victim and also a potent symbol of the corruption that plagues the Danish royal court. Ophelia, she says, is little more than an object used by her father and others for political and other purposes, while Ophelia herself is unable to resist becoming tainted by the evil of her abusers.

The truth is that Ophelia was a disreputable young woman. . . . She was foredoomed to it by her father [who failed to shield her from the corruption plaguing the court]. . . . The girl is not to be kept out of harm's way. She is a card that can be played [by ambitious men]. . . . Surely Ophelia is one of the few authentic portraits of . . . the poor little girls who were sacrificed to family ambition in the days when a court was a cat's cradle of conspiracies. . . . The picture of Ophelia shows that Shakespeare . . . was great in pity, that rare emotion. He shows the poor little creature, whom the court has robbed of her honesty, receiving no compensation for the loss, but being driven to madness and done to death. . . . It was the whole court that had destroyed her, which abandons principle for . . . politics, for intrigue, because of its too urgent sense that it must survive at all costs. . . . It is Shakespeare's contention that the whole of the court is corrupt. Society is corrupt.[89]

Of all the main characters, says West, only Hamlet is able to rise above the mire of this corruption, yet even he does so only in his last moments on the polluted earth.

The Emblems of Death
When Hamlet slips away in those last moments, he joins his father in that mysterious, often dreaded realm that people call death. It is "the undiscovered country, from whose bourn / No traveler returns,"[90] the prince of Denmark says in the "To be or not to be" speech. Death is certainly one of the most important recurring themes in *Hamlet*, an unwanted reality that the characters find themselves dealing with both literally and symbolically on a regular basis. Shakespeare begins and ends the play with images of death—a dead man walking on the battlements in the opening scenes, and the corpse-littered

throne room in the finale. All told, nine of the play's main characters die (if one counts old King Hamlet, murdered shortly before the action begins), not to mention the unspecified number of people Fortinbras butchers in Poland.

Moreover, the play repeatedly emphasizes that all the characters, and indeed all human beings, are trapped in a never-ending cycle of birth and death. Perhaps the most obvious and famous example is the scene in which Hamlet converses with the chief gravedigger. In contemplating the rows of skulls the man unearths, Hamlet must confront his own ultimate end and thus his own mortality. He realizes that he too will one day end up like "poor Yorick," the court jester whose skull he holds in his hand. Even the mightiest of mortals must inevitably succumb to death in the end and thus become part of the cycle of "dust-to-dust." "If there is a final secret to be revealed about that 'undiscovered country' on

In a contemplative moment, Hamlet whispers to Yorick's skull. Suddenly, the young man finds himself confronted by the concept of his own mortality.

which Hamlet's imagination broods," says Shakespearean scholar Michael Neill,

> it is perhaps only the Gravedigger's spade that can recover it. For his digging lays bare the one thing we can say for certain lies hidden "within" the mortal show of the flesh—the emblems of Death himself [i.e., skull and bones] . . . who shadows each of us. If there is a better story . . . it is, the play tells us, one that cannot finally be told; for it exists on the other side of language. . . . The great and frustrating achievement of this play, its most ingenious and tormenting trick, the source of its endlessly belabored mystery, is to persuade us that such a story might exist, while demonstrating its irreducible hiddenness. . . . The story of our lives, the play wryly acknowledges, is always the wrong story; but the rest, after all, is silence.[91]

Notes

Introduction: Hamlet Never Rests

1. Laurence Olivier, *On Acting*. New York: Simon and Schuster, 1986, pp. 76–77.
2. Quoted in Norrie Epstein, *The Friendly Shakespeare: A Thoroughly Painless Guide to the Best of the Bard*. New York: Viking Penguin, 1993, p. 336.
3. Michael Pennington, *Hamlet: A User's Guide*. New York: Proscenium, 1996, pp. 4–5.
4. Quoted in Mary Z. Maher, *Modern Hamlets and Their Soliloquies*. Iowa City: University of Iowa Press, 1992, p. 22.

Chapter 1: The Life, Times, and Works of William Shakespeare

5. Gareth Evans and Barbara Lloyd Evans, *The Shakespeare Companion*. New York: Scribner's, 1978, p. 25.
6. Evans and Evans, *Shakespeare Companion*, p. 17.
7. The date of his christening is registered as April 26, 1564. Since it was then customary to baptize an infant no later than the first Sunday or holy day following its birth, most scholars favor April 22 or 23 as Shakespeare's birth date. Regarding the end of his life, the date of his burial is known—April 25, 1616—and when the burial customs of the time are considered, April 23 seems a likely date for his death.
8. Karl J. Holzknecht, *The Backgrounds of Shakespeare's Plays*. New York: American, 1950, pp. 33–34.
9. William Shakespeare, *The Merry Wives of Windsor*, act 4, scene 1, lines 57–61, 74–78.
10. John F. Andrews, "The Past Is Prologue," in Wim Coleman, ed., *Othello*. Logan, IA: Perfection Form, 1987, pp. viii–ix.
11. A. A. Mendilow, "The Elizabethan Theater," in A. A. Mendilow and Alice Shalvi, *The World and Art of Shakespeare*. New York: Daniel Davey, 1967, pp. 26–27.
12. Evans and Evans, *Shakespeare Companion*, p. 21.
13. François Laroque, *The Age of Shakespeare*. New York: Harry N. Abrams, 1993, p. 39.

14. Quoted in Alice Shalvi, "Life of Shakespeare," in Mendilow and Shalvi, *World and Art of Shakespeare*, p. 9.

15. Ronald Watkins, *On Producing Shakespeare*. New York: Benjamin Blom, 1964, pp. 18–20.

16. Samuel Schoenbaum, *William Shakespeare: A Compact Documentary Life*. New York: Oxford University Press, 1977, p. 308.

17. Harry Levin, ed., *The Riverside Shakespeare*. Boston: Houghton Mifflin, 1974, p. 1.

Chapter 2: The Original Sources and Performance History of *Hamlet*

18. Epstein, *The Friendly Shakespeare*, p. 308.

19. Phyllis Abrahms and Alan Brody, introduction to Michael Martin, ed., *Hamlet*. New York: Prestige, 1968, p. xxi.

20. The name Hamlet is a form of Amleth, the non-Latinized version of Amlethus.

21. Introduction to G. R. Hibbard, ed., *Hamlet*. New York: Oxford University Press, 1987, p. 11.

22. The classic modern study of this vanished play and the possible identity of its author appears in Fredson T. Bowers, *Elizabethan Revenge Tragedy, 1587–1642*. Princeton, NJ: Princeton University Press, 1940.

23. Introduction to Susanne L. Wofford, ed., *William Shakespeare: Hamlet*. Boston: Bedford Books of St. Martin's Press, 1994, pp. 15–16.

24. Quoted in Samuel Thurber and A. B. de Mille, eds., *Hamlet*. Boston: Allyn and Bacon, 1922, p. 169.

25. Quoted in introduction to Robert Hapgood, ed., *Hamlet, Prince of Denmark*. New York: Cambridge University Press, 1999, p. 15.

26. Quoted in Hapgood, *Hamlet*, p. 19.

27. Quoted in Hapgood, *Hamlet*, p. 19.

28. Quoted in Martin, *Hamlet*, p. xxxii.

29. Quoted in Hapgood, *Hamlet*, p. 47.

30. Maher, *Modern Hamlets*, pp. 2, 18.

31. Actor-composer-writer Richard Sterne, who had a small part in this famous production of the play, secretly taped some private

rehearsals in which Gielgud and Burton worked alone on motivation, vocal techniques, and other aspects of the performance. Later, Sterne obtained Gielgud's and Burton's permission to make it public and the material, along with descriptions of other rehearsals, was published as Richard L. Sterne, *John Gielgud Directs Richard Burton in* Hamlet: *A Journal of Rehearsals.* New York: Random House, 1967. It remains a priceless record of a controversial and memorable version of Hamlet.

Chapter 3: The Story Told in Shakespeare's *Hamlet*

32. William Shakespeare, *Hamlet,* act 1, scene 1, line 49, quoted in Louis B. Wright and Virginia A. Lamar, eds., *The Tragedy of Hamlet, Prince of Denmark.* New York: Simon and Schuster, 1958.

33. *Hamlet* 1.1.62.

34. *Hamlet* 1.2.72–75.

35. *Hamlet* 1.2.143–64.

36. *Hamlet* 1.4.42.

37. *Hamlet* 1.5.45–46.

38. *Hamlet* 1.5.93–95.

39. *Hamlet* 2.2.207.

40. *Hamlet* 2.2.222–23.

41. *Hamlet* 2.2.311–18.

42. *Hamlet* 2.2.544–45.

43. *Hamlet* 2.2.596–613.

44. *Hamlet* 3.1.86–91.

45. *Hamlet* 3.1.130–31, 157.

46. *Hamlet* 3.1.170–71.

47. *Hamlet* 3.2.281.

48. *Hamlet* 3.3.39–41.

49. *Hamlet* 4.5.146–47.

50. *Hamlet* 4.7.157–62.

51. *Hamlet* 4.7.193–201.

52. *Hamlet* 5.1.136–61.

53. *Hamlet* 5.1.177–85.

54. *Hamlet* 5.2.329–30.

55. *Hamlet* 5.2.333–34, 340.

56. *Hamlet* 5.2.378–79, 384.

57. *Hamlet* 5.2.385–86.

58. *Hamlet* 5.2.428, 435.

Chapter 4: The Principal Characters Appearing in *Hamlet*

59. *Hamlet* 1.4.100.

60. Pennington, *Hamlet: A User's Guide*, p. 154.

61. *Hamlet* 3.3.58.

62. Peter Quennell and Hamish Johnson, *Who's Who in Shakespeare*. New York: William Morrow, 1973, p. 66.

63. *Hamlet* 5.2.420–21.

64. Rebecca Smith, "A Heart Cleft in Twain: The Dilemma of Shakespeare's Gertrude," in Carolyn R. S. Lenz et al., eds., *The Woman's Part: Feminist Criticism of Shakespeare*. Urbana: University of Illinois Press, 1980, p. 195.

65. It is possible that one of Shakespeare's reasons for portraying Gertrude as innocent and sympathetic was that, at the time *Hamlet* was first performed, Anne of Denmark was about to (or had recently) become queen of England, so it was the polite and expedient thing to do.

66. *Hamlet* 1.5.66–71, 81–82.

67. *Hamlet* 1.1.163.

68. Introduction to Philip Edwards, ed., *Hamlet, Prince of Denmark*. New York: Cambridge University Press, 1985, pp. 44, 61.

69. Pennington, *Hamlet: A User's Guide*, p. 176.

70. *Hamlet* 5.1.115–24.

71. Quoted in Maher, *Modern Hamlets*, p. 43.

72. *Hamlet* 3.2.72–75.

73. *Hamlet* 5.2.385–87.

74. *Hamlet* 5.2.84–85.

75. *Hamlet* 1.3.105–106.

76. Pennington, *Hamlet: A User's Guide*, pp. 162–63.

Chapter 5: Exploring the Basic Truths of the Human Experience

77. Abrahms and Brody, in Martin, *Hamlet*, pp. xviii–xix.

78. Marvin Rosenberg, *The Masks of Hamlet*. Newark: University of Delaware Press, 1992, p. xvi.

79. Quoted in Epstein, *The Friendly Shakespeare*, p. 343.

80. Michael Goldman, "Hamlet and Our Problems," in David S. Kastan, ed., *Critical Essays on Shakespeare's Hamlet*. New York: Simon and Schuster, 1995, p. 51.

81. *Hamlet* 1.2.135–38.

82. *Hamlet* 2.2.311–12.

83. *Hamlet* 3.1.64.

84. *Hamlet* 3.1.156.

85. *Hamlet* 2.2.313–14, 319–23.

86. *Hamlet* 2.2.555.

87. Salvador de Madariaga, *On Hamlet*. London: Frank Cass, 1964, p. 106.

88. Rebecca West, *The Court and the Castle*. New Haven, CT: Yale University Press, 1957, p. 17.

89. West, *The Court and the Castle*, pp. 18–26.

90. *Hamlet* 3.1.87–88.

91. Michael Neill, "*Hamlet*: A Modern Perspective," in Barbara A. Mowat and Paul Werstine, eds., *Hamlet*. New York: Simon and Schuster, 1992, pp. 325–26.

For Further Exploration

92. Quoted in Dimitri Shostakovich, *Testimony: The Memoirs of Dimitri Shostakovich*. Trans. Antonina W. Bouis. London: Faber, 1981, p. 84.

93. Rosenberg, *The Masks of Hamlet*, p. 70.

For Further Exploration

Below are some suggestions for themes or essays to write about Shakespeare's *Hamlet*, along with some related creative projects.

1. Cite some possible reasons why the Ghost suddenly vanishes when the cock crows and dawn approaches. *See also:* Prosser, *Hamlet and Revenge*, chapters 4 and 5.

2. What do Hamlet, Laertes, and Fortinbras all have in common? Also, what are some of their differences? *See also:* Pennington, *Hamlet: A User's Guide*, part 3.

3. What if all the plays ever written disappeared except for William Shakespeare's *Hamlet*, which somehow miraculously survived? This was the thought-provoking question asked by the great early-twentieth-century Russian stage director Vsevolod Meyerhold. His answer: "All the theaters in the world would be saved. They could all put on *Hamlet* and be successful."[92] Explain what you think Meyerhold meant by this statement. *See also:* Foakes, "The Reception of *Hamlet*," in *Hamlet and Its Afterlife*.

4. Find Hamlet's seven soliloquies. In each case, first explain the context, that is, tell what is happening in the play at that moment; second, in your own words briefly summarize what the character actually says in the speech. *See also:* Maher, *Modern Hamlets and Their Soliloquies*.

5. How is Ophelia used and abused by the powerful, ambitious men around her? Does she herself become infected with the corruption that pervades the royal court in which she lives? If so, how does it happen? *See also:* West, *The Court and the Castle*, chapter 1.

6. Consider Hamlet's mother, Gertrude. "Since she seems so seldom to assert herself verbally, and initially to submit to anything Claudius asks or demands," scholar Marvin Rosenberg points out, "she has been seen by critics for well over a century as weak and passive."[93] Look at some of Gertrude's scenes and speeches and find some evidence of a stronger, more assertive Gertrude. Cite some of her specific lines or actions to support your argument. *See also:* "Gertrude" in Rosenberg, *The Masks of Hamlet*; Smith, "A Heart Cleft in Twain: The Dilemma of Shakespeare's Gertrude," in Lenz et al., eds., *The Woman's Part: Feminist Criticism of Shakespeare*; and O'Brien, "Rewriting Gertrude," in *Hamlet and Its Afterlife*.

7. Why does Hamlet delay so long in achieving his revenge? This is a question that has been asked thousands of times since the play

was first written and there is no definitive answer. Support your theory by referencing the play. *See also:* Goldman, "Hamlet and Our Problems," in Kastan, ed., *Critical Essays on Shakespeare's Hamlet*; and Wilson, *What Happens in Hamlet*.

8. Trace the performance history of *Hamlet* since Shakespeare's time, citing one or two of the most famous actors who played the title role in each century and briefly describing their individual approaches and appearances. *See also:* introductions to Martin, ed., *Hamlet*, and Hapgood, ed., *Hamlet, Prince of Denmark*.

9. How is Hamlet affected by his Christian beliefs? How do they keep him from acting more like a traditional hero, who would immediately seek out and punish the person who murdered his father? *See also:* "Hamlet and Christianity" in Cantor, *Shakespeare: Hamlet*.

10. List all of the characters that die in the play. In each case, tell what is happening at the time of his or her death, and why and how he or she dies. Why do you think Shakespeare has so many characters perish? Consider how Hamlet's examination of Yorick's skull in the Gravedigger scene explores death as an inevitable, universal experience. What commentary is Shakespeare making about death? *See also:* Neill, "*Hamlet*: A Modern Perspective," in Mowat and Werstine, eds., *Hamlet*.

11. How old is Hamlet? Shakespeare does not tell us exactly in the play, but certain lines and speeches give hints. Cite some of this evidence to back up your argument for his age. *See also:* "Hamlet's Age," in de Madariaga, *On Hamlet*.

12. Read Tom Stoppard's play *Rosencrantz and Guildenstern Are Dead*. Compare and contrast it to Shakespeare's *Hamlet*, citing some of the ways that Stoppard used material from the original and also some of the effective ways he used new material of his own invention. *See also:* Stoppard, *Rosencrantz and Guildenstern Are Dead*.

13. Rent and watch the videos of the 1948 film version of *Hamlet*, directed by and starring Laurence Olivier, and the 1990 film, directed by Franco Zeffirelli and starring Mel Gibson. Compare the two films. How did Olivier use black-and-white photography to create atmosphere? What are some of the differences in atmosphere created by the use of color in Zeffirelli's version? Compare the acting styles of Olivier and Gibson. Though both men can be described as athletic Hamlets, how do their approaches to the role differ? How do the characterizations of Claudius, Gertrude, and Ophelia differ in the two films? Explain why you think one

film is more effective than the other or why they are equally effective. *See also:* "Olivier's *Hamlet* and Other Screen Versions," in Hapgood, ed., *Hamlet, Prince of Denmark*; Biggs, "Hamlet and Gertrude on Screen," in *Hamlet and Its Afterlife;* and Kliman, *Hamlet: Film, Television, and Audio Performance.*

14. Choose two or more scenes from Shakespeare's *Hamlet*, assemble some interested friends, and stage them, if possible capturing them on video. (It is not necessary to use sets, costumes, or elaborate props and lighting effects; concentrate instead on understanding the lines and making the characters and their interactions believable.) Afterward, jot down some of your reactions to the experience. What did it teach you about Shakespeare? About the difficulties of staging his plays? About the value of drama as a way of expressing human emotions and examining human problems? For those who are especially ambitious, have a teacher, drama coach, experienced actor, or some other qualified person review your performance and then use his or her critique as a guide in revising and restaging it. *See also:* Davison, *Hamlet: Text and Performance;* and Pennington's *Hamlet: A User's Guide*, which is highly recommended for anyone trying to perform this play.

Appendix of Criticism

The Ghost's Believability

The believability of the Ghost varies from one production of Hamlet *to another, depending on the stature of the actor playing it and the lighting and other stage effects employed. Shakespearean scholar Salvador de Madariaga comments on what Shakespeare himself did to make the Ghost believable.*

Shakespeare's own attitude towards the Ghost is no mystery. About ghosts in general he was a sceptic with an open mind—just as Horatio before the actual apparition convinced him. The proof of this view is the way in which he makes the four witnesses react to the vision each in his own manner; which shows that he, Shakespeare, was free, not only from belief but from disbelief as well. But about the particular Ghost in *Hamlet*, Shakespeare's opinion was that it was an excellent piece of dramatic mechanism which had to impress his audience by its "reality", but which could not impress the author at all, since he was making it up.

His problem, therefore, was to make his audience believe in his Ghost even though he did not believe in it himself. He went about it ably enough, for his dramatic skill was unrivalled, provided he took trouble enough and was not betrayed by his buoyant spirits into some antic. And sure enough the Ghost becomes real even before it has spoken, thanks to the consummate skill lavished on its first two visitations and on the talk before and after, on the platform.

Things, however, begin to go awry precisely at the most solemn moment. The dialogue between Hamlet and his father's spirit has just begun when a whiff of flippancy and fun passes through Shakespeare's mind. It is irrepressible. And so, in the midst of the utmost solemnity, incongruous humour bursts forth—a humour which is not in the characters, but in the poet behind them.

Ghost: My hour is almost come,

When I to sulphurous and tormenting flames

Must render up myself.

Hamlet: Alas, poor ghost.

This is Shakespeare laughing with Shakespeare through Hamlet, just as Hamlet, in the play, laughs with Hamlet through Polonius. True, it might be interpreted as a Protestant hint at the crowd on the laughability of the belief in Purgatory; and those who attach a particular importance to the differences between Protestants and Catholics on the subject of ghosts might have availed themselves of this detail.

This view, however, requires that Hamlet II should be protestant and Hamlet I catholic; and it puts too nice a distinction on Shakespeare's words. In what concerns this particular episode, Hamlet's "Alas, poor Ghost!" can have no such theological background or intention, for a second quiet chuckle comes from the poet to warn us that he is not really poking fun at Catholic theology, but at the Ghost itself.

Ghost: Pity me not, but lend thy serious hearing

To what I shall unfold.

To which Hamlet makes this truly comic answer:

Speak: I am bound to hear.

Salvador de Madariaga, *On Hamlet*. London: Frank Cass, 1964.

A Study in the Passion of Grief

According to this analysis by the late and noted literary scholar Lily B. Campbell, one of the main emotions driving the actions of the play is grief, which many of the characters are unable to contain.

The play of *Hamlet* is concerned with the story of three young men—Hamlet, Fortinbras, and Laertes—each called upon to mourn the death of a father, each feeling himself summoned to revenge wrongs suffered by his father. Grief in each for the loss of his father is succeeded by the desire for revenge. But each must act according to the dictates of his own temperament and his own humour.

The fundamental problem that Shakespeare undertook to answer in Hamlet, then, is the problem of the way men accept sorrow when it comes to them. And it is evident throughout the play that the grief of Fortinbras is being presented as a grief dominated by reason, while it is equally evident that the grief of Hamlet and Laertes is excessive grief leading to destruction. That Hamlet himself saw in these two other young men his own image, is of course, evident. . . .

In many respects and by nature Hamlet is like Fortinbras, but he has been changed by grief into something different. . . .

If my analysis is correct, then, *Hamlet* becomes a study in the passion of grief. In Hamlet himself it is passion which is not moderated by reason, a passion which will not yield to the consolations of philosophy. And being intemperate and excessive grief, Hamlet's grief is, therefore, the grief that makes memory fade, that makes reason fail in directing the will, that makes him guilty of sloth. Yet Hamlet is capable of an anger that demands revenge. His blood answered the ghost's first demand with a swift promise; he could offend Ophelia, kill Polonius, escape on shipboard, insult Laertes, even kill the King in moments of unreasonable passion, but

What to ourselves in passion we propose,

The passion ending, doth the purpose lose,

The violence of either grief or joy

Their own enactures with themselves destroy.

Because in our own day we are sentimental about grief and those that grieve, it is hard for us to get the Renaissance point of view in regard to grief, a point of view which was inherited from the Middle Ages as well as from the older classical philosophy. Shakespeare did not fail to see and to show the essential humanness of grief in its passionate refusal of the consolations of philosophy. Neither did he fail to show the destruction which followed Hamlet's slothfulness [slowness] in executing what his reason had judged and commanded him to do. Nor did he fail to show the destruction that came from his passionate and rash action when he acted from passion and not from reason.

Laertes, too, was the victim of excessive grief, but his grief was that which moved to rage. He, too, acted from passion and not from reason. Even in his killing of Hamlet he acted against the dictates of his own conscience, having promised to do so under the influence of violent passion, moved by grief to hate and by hate to revenge.

Lily B. Campbell, *Shakespeare's Tragic Heroes: Slaves of Passion.* New York: Barnes and Noble, 1968, pp. 109–10, 144.

Hamlet's Six Most Famous Syllables

Marvin Rosenberg, a respected University of California drama professor, here muses about the wide variety of possible ways to speak and interpret what is surely Hamlet's most famous line.

To be, or not to be . . .

seems, especially after the first soliloquy's yearning for death, to ask: "to live or not to live?" (And so it has often been translated.) Unless (as critics enlarge the implication, and separate it from suicidal thought), in Hamlet's existential mind *to be* . . . means "to act, to live fully;" and *not to be* means "to sleep and feed, no more." Conversely, *to be* has been taken to suggest merely existing, *not to be* something active, participant. Or is this Hamlet's detached, philosophical speculation on the nature of being? How creative Shakespearean interpreters can be!

The six monosyllables make a question, but are not always asked as one. Their line has been said fiercely by a Hamlet on the point of decision; softly and slowly by one lost in meditation. . . . The stress varies with the speaker. It is often "To be, or *not* to be," or "To *be*, or *not* to *be*?" It has been "*To* be, or not *to be*?" The line has been spoken quickly, feelingly, the words powered by emotion. One actor made it "To be or not? . . . *To be!*"—a declaration of continuance. *That, is, the* and *question* have been stressed; sometimes, intensely, all the words. Try it.

Even if, as has been suggested, the *question* might have been a standard one for discussion, Hamlet's situation makes it urgently his own. If he is deep in thought, his second question may seem an outgrowth of the first, or a parallel to it. Together they demand a solution to a moral issue crucial to Hamlet.

> Whether 'tis nobler in the *mind* to *suffer*
>
> The slings and arrows of *outrageous fortune* . . .

Nobility is at stake; though of what kind the actor-reader must decide. Is it nobler to suffer? Or nobler to suffer in the mind, not speak—break my heart, for I must hold my tongue? . . .

Are there *two* dilemmas? "Live or die?" "Suffer or resist?" Is this a scholar's mind indulging in a debate on essential human enigmas? A revenger at the point of setting his trap, suddenly preferring to think rather than act? Tranced in inertia? A despairing young man more than ever drawn toward a dissolution of the flesh?

> Marvin Rosenberg, *The Masks of Hamlet.* Newark: University of
> Delaware Press, 1992, pp. 475–77.

The Formality of Court Speech

The setting in which Hamlet's story takes place is an integral element of the story. As noted Shakespearean scholar R. A. Foakes suggests, the nature of that setting is shaped in large degree by the formality of the language used at the royal court.

One of the most prominent features of *Hamlet* is the ceremonious and stately diction of the court. When the major characters speak in public they have generally a leisured way of speaking, using many words to say little, freely amplifying and illustrating, as when . . . Hamlet welcomes the news that the players are coming:

> He that plays the king shall be welcome; his majesty shall have tribute of me; the adventurous knight shall use his foil and target; the lover shall not sigh gratis.

(II, ii, 332–5)

This rhetorical way of speaking appears in the devices of Hamlet's excuse to Laertes, "Was't Hamlet wrong'd Laertes? Never Hamlet", in the marked pompousness of the verse Rosencrantz and Guildenstern use for intercourse with the King, and in the formal balance of such lines as:

> *King.* Thanks, Rosencrantz and gentle Guildenstern.
>
> *Queen.* Thanks, Guildenstern and gentle Rosencrantz. . . .

(II, ii, 33–4)

It is a 'public' manner of speaking, which tends to sound similar in the mouths of different characters, and preserves an outward stateliness and formality in the court.

While it is more or less habitual to the practised courtiers like Polonius, Laertes or Osric, it may also afford a screen behind which truth can be concealed, and there is a strong contrast between the public and private speech of several characters, notably Claudius and Hamlet. Claudius, for instance, has a more direct and personal manner when praying, trying to obtain information, or plotting with an accomplice, but for the most part he is shown speaking in public. . . . It is the vice of Polonius that he exaggerates the worst features of the style, and on this occasion the King and Queen are eager for fact and have no time for rhetoric; "More matter, with less art", cries Gertrude.

Other elements in the play contribute to this formal, rhetorical tone. There is endless moralizing. . . . Claudius is ready with long-winded and commonplace advice for Hamlet, and so are Polonius for Laertes, Laertes for Ophelia, and Hamlet for the players. Many characters besides Polonius are stored with proverbs or 'sentences'. Set speeches and formal descriptions abound, such as Horatio's account of events in Denmark, the Ghost's tale of the murder, Hamlet's speech on man, Gertrude's description of Ophelia's death, Hamlet's story of the sea-battle. . . .

All these formal elements are present in some of the 'public' speeches, such as the court flattery of Rosencrantz. The pomp and spaciousness of such diction is part of the atmosphere of *Hamlet*. The court of Elsinore is a place of ostensible stateliness and nobility; affairs of state, dealings with ambassadors, preparations for war, enter into the action, and many of the 'pictures' the play presents on the stage, its direct images, are static or nearly so, like the pictorial effect of the dumb-show in the play scene, of Hamlet's contemplation of Claudius praying, of the pictures in the closet-scene, and of the skulls in the graveyard-scene.

> R. A. Foakes, "Hamlet and the Court of Elsinore," in Allardyce Nicoll, ed., *Shakespeare Survey*, no. 9. Cambridge, England: Cambridge University Press, 1956, pp. 36–37.

The Actors Bring the Play to Life

Popular stage and film actor Kevin Kline has played the title role in Shakespeare's Hamlet *on more than one occasion. He also directed a production of the play in 1990. Here, he stresses the importance of the director allowing the actors to use their natural gifts and instincts to bring the play to life.*

I wanted the play to be about *these* people in *this* situation—it's not about thrones and crowns and pageantry. If we make the actors create the play, they'll have to use their voices and their bodies and the words, the poetry, to tell the story. In that tiny space, there was not room for much else. So, the production was simple, stripped down, modern dress—clothes which say Student, King, Queen, Secretary of State, Daughter, Soldier. As for the period, this is a story in which kings squared off in single combat to decide the fate of the nation, and yet by the end of the play, there is a courtly rapier-and-dagger duel, so let's just not worry about anachronism because Shakespeare didn't. Let's give the actors clothes that they're not going to pose and "be Shakespearean" in—where they will have to talk to one another and be *real*. I wanted to use the whole vocabulary of acting—of naturalism and also of the most sweeping epic poetic drama. That space can hold great raging tempestuous speeches and you can also speak as I am speaking now and still have presence. . . .

I had to live up to my own credo—that actors must assume the authorship of their own work. I made it clear at the outset that we are the ones who tell the story every night. It's not the director. I was careful to get actors who would take that responsibility. One who says, "Well, this is a job and I do what the director tells me" is not an actor I'm interested in. I want an actor who has a personal connection to the play and to his or her role. They would demand of me "Why?" And I would tell them "try it this way because then the scene becomes more about this than about that—do you agree? See what I mean?" So it was a *dialogue* with them. Of course, there were times when I simply wanted to say, "Just do it like I told you." I had to stop myself from that because I didn't want them betraying themselves as actors. If the bit of business or a way of saying a line is not ultimately *their decision*, then the acting won't be that good or that full. What's riveting when you watch a good actor—if it's an action that he or she has arrived at and has some ownership in it, then it has an air of instinctive commitment. It will come alive in a much richer way than if the actor is a puppet.

Quoted in Mary Z. Maher, *Modern Hamlets and Their Soliloquies.* Iowa City: University of Iowa Press, 1992, pp. 177, 179.

A Psychological Approach to Hamlet

The late, great actor Laurence Olivier, who directed and starred in the 1948 Oscar-winning film of Hamlet, *was famous for his psychological approach to the play and its title character. Specifically, as he explains in this excerpt from his book,* On Acting, *he saw the possibility that Hamlet had an unhealthy attraction to his mother, the queen.*

Hamlet is pound for pound, in my opinion, the greatest play ever written. It towers above everything else in dramatic literature. It gives us great climaxes, shadows and shades, yet contains occasional moments of high comedy. Every time you read a line it can be a new discovery. You can play it and play it as many times as the opportunity occurs and still not get to the bottom of its box of wonders. It can trick you round false corners and into culs-de-sac, or take you by the seat of your pants and hurl you across the stars. It can give you moments of unknown joy, or cast you into the depths of despair. Once you have played it, it will devour you and obsess you for the rest of your life. It has me. I think each day about it. I'll never play him again, of course, but by God, I wish I could. . . .

Many years ago, when I was first to play Hamlet at the Old Vic, I went with Tyrone Guthrie, who was going to direct it, and Peggy Ashcroft, who was going to play Ophelia (but for some regrettable reason wasn't able to), to see Professor Ernest Jones, the great psychiatrist, who had made an exhaustive study of Hamlet from his own professional point of view and was wonderfully enlightening. . . .

We talked and talked. He believed that Hamlet was a prime sufferer from the Oedipus complex. There are many signals along the line to show his inner involvement with his mother. One of them is his excessive devotion to his father. Nobody's that fond of his father unless he feels guilty about his mother, however subconscious that guilt may be. Hamlet's worship of his father is manufactured, assumed; he needs it to cover up his subconscious guilt. The Oedipus complex may, indeed, be responsible for a formidable share of all that is wrong with Hamlet. I myself am only too happy to allow to be added to Shakespeare's other acknowledged gifts an intuitive understanding of psychology. Why not? He was the world's greatest man. . . .

I can't remember if Jones came to see the production; I don't think he did. But I warned him that he would not find the Oedipal theory overt, though, of course, it would be there. He said, "I wouldn't suggest you should make it overt, as long as you know about it. That's the important point. You're not supposed to tell the audience with every wink and nod that one of the reasons for your present predicament is that you wish you were still hanging on your mother's tits." A very entertaining man.

Laurence Olivier, *On Acting*. New York: Simon and Schuster, 1986, pp. 76–78.

Chaos and Decay Counterbalanced by Intelligence and Wit

Former University of Cambridge scholar John Holloway makes the point that even when the events of Hamlet *degenerate into madness, intrigue, chaos, and murder, the play still shines with elements of intelligence and wit, especially in the speeches of Hamlet and Polonius.*

[The] whole movement in the action is symbolized in the spectacular tableau (it comes towards the close of Act V scene i), where the two young men of the play, soon to fight a duel using an unbaited and poisoned weapon, stand struggling in the open grave, surrounded by the rituals of death by suicide. But in thus tracing this movement through metaphor and symbol and fantasy and spectacle, we should remember that these things are not its primary vehicle; they help to make the movement pervasive and potent, but it is one which is embodied in the first instance in the action itself.

There are many plays in which, to put the matter baldly, the case of the *dramatis personae* gets worse as the play goes on. In *Hamlet* this occurs, in two ways, with a distinctive nuance. To begin with, over its whole length the play shows this degeneration into universal violence, conspiracy and chaos within the frame of a brilliant, exhilarating and yet (when once it is seen) disturbing and indeed fearful paradox. The world of *Hamlet*, as it declines into tragedy and chaos, yet maintains one part of itself always in a condition of exuberantly febrile life. Whatever else decays, there remains an incessant play and thrust of frenzied intrigue, of plot and counterplot, and on the surface of this, as its overt counterpart, a scintillating texture of intelligence and wit. Largely, this is the incomparable contribution of Hamlet himself; but not only so. Polonius plays his part at the beginning, Osric at the end. The grave-yard scene is almost an emblem of this paradox within the play: Hamlet's last and most extravagant ingenuities flash about that universal death, real on the stage and imagined by the actors, which is the state towards which the people of the play are heading all the time. This staggering hypertrophy of intelligence provides one large part of the delight and excitement; but another part, not exuberant, but none the less powerful for that, lies in our supervening awareness of how this play of wit iridesces [glows] upon the great *caput mortuum* [worthless residue] which is coming into focus everywhere below it. Here is something surely unique in Shakespeare.

John Holloway, *The Story of the Night: Studies in Shakespeare's Major Tragedies.* Lincoln: University of Nebraska Press, 1961, pp. 32–33.

Two Hapless, Doomed Characters

It might be argued that Hamlet is, from the beginning, a doomed character. His visiting school friends, Rosencrantz and Guildenstern, certainly are doomed, as suggested in this brief overview of their "hapless" characters by noted actor and scholar Michael Pennington.

These days, ROSENCRANTZ and GUILDENSTERN would be sent back to the author for further work, perhaps with a suggestion that the two parts could be combined into one. Why two salaries? If

Shakespeare wanted a friend for Hamlet as corrupted as Horatio is loyal, how about Rosenstern?

Is there really any difference between these two? It is difficult to see it as you watch. Without the complementary feed-and-punch rhythm of the true double-act, they are more a duet for perfectly matched voices, and something about the hapless pair invites facetiousness. . . .

They start as they mean to go on, introducing themselves with the same voice and in the same rhythm:

ROSENCRANTZ: Both your majesties

Might by the sovereign power you have of us

Put your dread pleasures more into command

Than to entreaty.

GUILDENSTERN: But we both obey

And here give up ourselves in the full bent

To lay our service freely at your feet

To be commanded.

—whereupon the Queen makes a joke about their identity. It is not a promising start for two hopeful young actors anxious to prove their distinctiveness.

When they report back things are little better:

ROSENCRANTZ: He does confess he feels himself distracted

But from what cause he will by no means speak.

GUILDENSTERN: Nor do we find him forward to be sounded

But with a crafty madness keeps aloof

When we would bring him on to some confession

Of his true state.

Then they plunge into the action, to be whirled about by it until they are dead, getting all the worst jobs and being blamed by everyone, ever less distinct from each other: it seems that their purpose is purely antiphonal, one voice split into two. . . .

It is of course an unenviable position in any time or culture to be plucked out to help in some domestic crisis affecting the Royal Family: and Rosencrantz and Guildenstern suffer a more or less permanent anxiety. Their formality when brought face to face with the monarch contrasts well with their easy prose rhythms with Hamlet, the only other character they speak to for more than a moment: there's a deal of undergraduate silliness in their first encounter with him, but they do at least sound like human beings. However, they will never be able to relax with Hamlet either, since, apart from his justified mistrust, he may at any moment sell them a dummy—a great wrong-footer, he pulls rank on them, judges them mercilessly, and finally destroys them. To this sense of inevitable casualty the actors have to hang on tight, through their various protests, acquiescences, uneasy perceptions of divided loyalty; above all the two of them are not silly, certainly not campy, but decent men in over their heads. The news of their deaths:

HORATIO: So Guildenstern and Rosencrantz go to't.

should carry a reproof from Horatio and bring a silence to the theatre.

Michael Pennington, *Hamlet: A User's Guide.*
New York: Proscenium, 1996, pp. 182–84.

Chronology

12th Century
The *Historica Danica* ("Chronicles of the Danish Realm"), the original story of Hamlet, is written.

1543
Polish astronomer Nicolaus Copernicus introduces the idea of a sun- rather than earth-centered universe in his *On the Revolutions.*

1557
William Shakespeare's parents, John Shakespeare and Mary Arden, are married.

1558
Elizabeth I becomes queen of England, initiating the Elizabethan age.

1564
William Shakespeare is born in the village of Stratford in central England; his noted contemporary, writer Christopher Marlowe, is also born.

1572
Playwright Ben Jonson, who will later become a rival of Shakespeare's, is born.

1576
London's first public theater, called the Theatre, opens.

1577
Raphael Holinshed's *Chronicles*, which will become the source for many of Shakespeare's plays, appears.

1577–1580
Englishman Sir Francis Drake sails around the world.

1582
William Shakespeare marries Anne Hathaway.

1585
Shakespeare's twins, Hamnet and Judith, are born.

ca. 1586
English playwright Thomas Kyd writes *The Spanish Tragedy*, a work that popularizes the "revenge tragedy" theatrical genre in which Shakespeare will later write *Hamlet.*

1587
Queen Elizabeth executes her rival, Mary, queen of Scots; at about this time Shakespeare leaves Stratford and heads for London to pursue a career in the theater.

1588
England wins a major victory over Spain by defeating the mighty Spanish Armada.

ca. 1590–1593
Shakespeare writes *Richard III; The Comedy of Errors; Henry VI, Parts 1, 2, and 3;* and *Titus Andronicus,* his first revenge play.

1594
Shakespeare joins the newly formed Lord Chamberlain's Men theatrical company.

ca. 1594–1600
Shakespeare writes *The Taming of the Shrew; The Two Gentlemen of Verona; The Merry Wives of Windsor; Twelfth Night; Richard II; Henry IV, Parts 1 and 2; Henry V;* and *Julius Caesar.*

1597
Shakespeare buys New Place, the largest home in Stratford.

1598–1599
The Globe Theater opens; Shakespeare owns one-eighth of its profits.

1600
In Italy, the church burns priest Giordano Bruno at the stake for advocating the idea that the stars are other suns, each having its own planets.

ca. 1600–1601
Hamlet is written and first performed.

ca. 1601–1607
Shakespeare writes his great tragedies, *Othello, King Lear, Macbeth,* and *Antony and Cleopatra.*

1603
Queen Elizabeth dies; James I becomes king of England; the English conquer Ireland; the first, shortest, and most corrupt quarto of *Hamlet* appears.

1604
The Second Quarto, now called the "good quarto," of *Hamlet* is published.

1607
English settlers establish the colony of Jamestown, giving England a permanent foothold in North America.

ca. 1608–1613
Shakespeare writes *Coriolanus*, *The Winter's Tale*, *Henry VIII*, and *The Two Noble Kinsmen*.

1610
Italian scholar Galileo Galilei points his newly built telescope at the planet Jupiter and discovers four orbiting moons, proving conclusively that all heavenly bodies do not revolve around the earth.

1611
The King James version of the Bible is published.

1616
Shakespeare dies.

1619
Richard Burbage, the great Elizabethan actor, and the first person ever to play Hamlet, dies.

1623
Anne Hathaway Shakespeare dies; the First Folio, a collection of Shakespeare's complete works, is published.

1663
The renowned English actor Thomas Betterton begins performing in *Hamlet*.

1742
David Garrick, one of the greatest actors of the eighteenth century, first tackles the role of Hamlet.

1759
Lewis Hallam becomes the first important American Hamlet.

1929
English actor Sir John Gielgud first plays Hamlet at London's Old Vic Theater; his interpretation of the role becomes the most acclaimed and influential of the twentieth century.

1937
English actor Sir Laurence Olivier, widely acknowledged as the greatest actor of the twentieth century, plays Hamlet onstage in London.

1948
Olivier releases his film version of *Hamlet*, which wins Academy Awards for best picture and actor.

1964
Gielgud directs popular actor Richard Burton in the role of Hamlet in a long-running New York production of the play; another popular actor, Christopher Plummer, plays Hamlet in a TV production shot on location at Elsinore Castle in Denmark.

1969
A film version of *Hamlet* starring Nicol Williamson in the title role is released.

1990
Popular star Mel Gibson plays Hamlet in a colorful film version directed by Franco Zeffirelli.

1997
English actor-director Kenneth Branagh releases a four-hour-long, uncut film version of *Hamlet*.

Works Consulted

A Sampling of Modern Editions of *Hamlet*

Philip Edwards, ed., *Hamlet, Prince of Denmark*. New York: Cambridge University Press, 1985.

Willard Farnham, ed., *The Tragedy of Hamlet, Prince of Denmark*. Baltimore: Penguin, 1961.

Robert Hapgood, ed., *Hamlet, Prince of Denmark*. New York: Cambridge University Press, 1999.

G. R. Hibbard, ed., *Hamlet*. New York: Oxford University Press, 1987.

Cyrus Hoy, ed., *Hamlet: An Authoritative Text, Intellectual Backgrounds, Extracts from the Sources, Essays in Criticism*. New York: W. W. Norton, 1963.

Harry Levin, ed., *The Riverside Shakespeare*. Boston: Houghton Mifflin, 1974.

Michael Martin, ed., *Hamlet*. New York: Prestige, 1968.

Barbara A. Mowat and Paul Werstine, eds., *Hamlet*. New York: Simon and Schuster, 1992.

Samuel Thurber and A. B. de Mille, eds., *Hamlet*. Boston: Allyn and Bacon, 1922.

Susanne L. Wofford, ed., *William Shakespeare: Hamlet*. Boston: Bedford Books of St. Martin's Press, 1994.

Louis B. Wright and Virginia A. Lamar, eds., *The Tragedy of Hamlet, Prince of Denmark*. New York: Simon and Schuster, 1958.

Analysis and Criticism of *Hamlet*

Paul Cantor, *Shakespeare:* Hamlet. New York: Cambridge University Press, 1989. A short but excellent study of the play, concentrating mainly on the title character's heroic qualities and how these are shaped by and conflict with his Christian upbringing.

Salvador de Madariaga, *On Hamlet*. London: Frank Cass, 1964. The author attempts to answer many of the questions that have often been posed about this complex and compelling play, including why the title character delays so long in enacting his revenge.

Hamlet and Its Afterlife (series of essays about the play), in Stanley Wells, ed., *Shakespeare Survey.* Cambridge, England: Cambridge University Press, 1993. These essays about the play, written by noted scholars including R. A. Foakes, Ellen J. O'Brien, and Murray Biggs, are perceptive and thought-provoking.

Ernest Jones, *Hamlet and Oedipus.* New York: W. W. Norton, 1949. Now a classic in Shakespearean studies, this book attempts to show that Hamlet suffers from a Freudian Oedipus complex and therefore has an underlying sexual desire for his mother. Will appeal mainly to scholars and Hamlet buffs.

David S. Kastan, ed., *Critical Essays on Shakespeare's Hamlet.* New York: Simon and Schuster, 1995. A very fine collection of essays about the play, with contributions by Michael Goldman, George T. Wright, Paul Werstine, and other noted Shakespearean scholars.

Mary Z. Maher, *Modern Hamlets and Their Soliloquies.* Iowa City: University of Iowa Press, 1992. This fascinating book examines some specific portrayals of Hamlet by famous actors, among them John Gielgud, Richard Burton, Ben Kingsley, and Kevin Kline. Highly recommended.

Michael Pennington, *Hamlet: A User's Guide.* New York: Proscenium, 1996. A wonderful, consistently perceptive, and enlightening guide to the play by a veteran of many productions of it. Very highly recommended for students, teachers, actors, and critics alike.

Eleanor Prosser, *Hamlet and Revenge.* Stanford, CA: Stanford University Press, 1967. This well-known study of one of the play's main themes, as well as how the play fits into the revenge play tradition, is still relevant and useful.

Marvin Rosenberg, *The Masks of Hamlet.* Newark: University of Delaware Press, 1992. A large, somewhat scholarly volume that contains a great deal of detailed analysis of the play's scenes, lines, themes, and characters. Will appeal mainly to scholars, stage directors and actors, and serious students of Shakespeare.

Rebecca West, *The Court and the Castle.* New Haven, CT: Yale University Press, 1957. West's well-known book about the play concentrates on the corruption and disease that "infects" Denmark's royal court and the people who inhabit it.

John Dover Wilson, *What Happens in Hamlet.* Cambridge, England: Cambridge University Press, 1964. Originally published in 1935, this perceptive and entertaining book is still one of the best general studies of the play and is highly recommended to all.

Filmed Versions of *Hamlet* and Other Shakespearean Plays

Brenda Cross, ed., *The Film* Hamlet: *A Record of Its Production.* London: Saturn, 1948. This interesting and entertaining volume is about the making of Laurence Olivier's film version of *Hamlet,* for which he received the Oscar for best actor.

Charles W. Eckert, *Focus on Shakespearean Films.* Englewood Cliffs, NJ: Prentice-Hall, 1972. A good general account of Shakespearean movies made up to the 1970s.

Bernice W. Kliman, Hamlet: *Film, Television, and Audio Performance.* Rutherford, NJ: Fairleigh Dickinson University Press, 1988. This is a commendable, informative summary of recorded Hamlets, including those of Laurence Olivier, Maurice Evans, Maximilian Schell, Christopher Plummer, Nicol Williamson, Richard Chamberlain, Derek Jacobi, and others.

Roger Manvell, *Shakespeare and the Film.* London: Debt, 1971. One of the best books ever written on the subject.

Shakespeare's Life, Theater, and Times

John C. Adams, *The Globe Playhouse: Its Design and Equipment.* Cambridge, MA: Harvard University Press, 1942. An indispensable mine of information about the theater used by Shakespeare and his colleagues and how it looked and operated.

Gerald E. Bentley, *Shakespeare: A Biographical Handbook.* Westport, CT: Greenwood, 1986. Contains valuable information about Shakespeare, his plays, and his society.

François Laroque, *The Age of Shakespeare.* New York: Harry N. Abrams, 1993. A short, entertaining sketch of Shakespeare's life and times, enhanced by many beautiful color drawings and photos.

Peter Levi, *The Life and Times of William Shakespeare.* New York: Henry Holt, 1989. One of the better Shakespeare biographies, written by a noted scholar.

Peter Quennell, *Shakespeare: A Biography.* Cleveland: World, 1963. This well-written synopsis of Shakespeare's life and work is by one of the most widely respected Shakespearean scholars.

A. L. Rowse, *Shakespeare the Man.* New York: Harper and Row, 1973. Another worthwhile biography of Shakespeare.

Other Notable Books Relating to Shakespeare and His Works

Isaac Asimov, *Asimov's Guide to Shakespeare.* New York: Avenel, 1978.

Charles Boyce, *Shakespeare: A to Z: The Essential Reference to His Plays, His Poems, His Life and Times, and More.* New York: Facts On File, 1990.

Andrew C. Bradley, *Shakespearean Tragedy.* New York: Viking Penguin, 1991.

Ivor Brown, *Shakespeare and the Actors.* New York: Coward McCann, 1970.

John R. Brown, *William Shakespeare: Writing for Performance.* New York: St. Martin's, 1996.

Lily B. Campbell, *Shakespeare's Tragic Heroes: Slaves of Passion.* New York: Barnes and Noble, 1968.

Edmund K. Chambers, *William Shakespeare: A Study of Facts and Problems.* New York: Oxford University Press, 1989.

Marchette Chute, *Shakespeare of London.* New York: E. P. Dutton, 1949.

Peter Davison, *Hamlet: Text and Performance.* Atlantic Highlands, NJ: Humanities Press, 1983.

Norrie Epstein, *The Friendly Shakespeare: A Thoroughly Painless Guide to the Best of the Bard.* New York: Viking Penguin, 1993.

Gareth Evans and Barbara Lloyd Evans, *The Shakespeare Companion.* New York: Scribner's, 1978.

M. D. Faber, *The Design Within: Psychoanalytic Approaches to Shakespeare.* New York: Science House, 1970.

R. A. Foakes, *Hamlet Versus Lear.* New York: Cambridge University Press, 1993.

Roland M. Frye, *Shakespeare's Life and Times: A Pictorial Record.* Princeton, NJ: Princeton University Press, 1967.

Brian Gibbons, *Shakespeare and Multiplicity.* Cambridge, England: Cambridge University Press, 1993.

John Gielgud, *An Actor and His Times.* London: Sidgwick and Jackson, 1979.

Harley Granville-Barker and G. B. Harrison, eds., *A Companion to Shakespeare Studies.* Cambridge, England: Cambridge University Press, 1959.

G. B. Harrison, *Elizabethan Plays and Players.* Ann Arbor: University of Michigan Press, 1956.

John Holloway, *The Story of the Night: Studies in Shakespeare's Major Tragedies*. Lincoln: University of Nebraska Press, 1961.

Karl J. Holzknecht, *The Backgrounds of Shakespeare's Plays*. New York: American, 1950.

Jack J. Jorgens, *Shakespeare on Film*. Bloomington: Indiana University Press, 1977.

François Laroque, *Shakespeare's Festive World: Elizabethan Seasonal Entertainment and the Professional Stage*. New York: Cambridge University Press, 1991.

Carolyn R. S. Lenz et al., eds., *The Woman's Part: Feminist Criticism of Shakespeare*. Urbana: University of Illinois Press, 1980.

Harry Levin, *The Question of Hamlet*. New York: Oxford University Press, 1959.

Maynard Mack Jr., *Killing the King: Three Studies in Shakespeare's Tragic Structure*. New Haven, CT: Yale University Press, 1973.

Dieter Mehl, *Shakespeare's Tragedies: An Introduction*. New York: Cambridge University Press, 1986.

A. A. Mendilow and Alice Shalvi, *The World and Art of Shakespeare*. New York: Daniel Davey, 1967.

Kenneth Muir and Samuel Schoenbaum, eds., *A New Companion to Shakespeare Studies*. Oxford, England: Oxford University Press, 1971.

Don Nardo, ed., *Readings on Hamlet*. San Diego: Greenhaven Press, 1999.

———, *Readings on Julius Caesar*. San Diego: Greenhaven Press, 1999.

———, *Readings on Othello*. San Diego: Greenhaven Press, 2000.

———, *Readings on Romeo and Juliet*. San Diego: Greenhaven Press, 1998.

Allardyce Nicoll, ed., *Shakespeare Survey*, no. 9. Cambridge, England: Cambridge University Press, 1956.

Laurence Olivier, *On Acting*. New York: Simon and Schuster, 1986.

Peter Quennell and Hamish Johnson, *Who's Who in Shakespeare*. New York: William Morrow, 1973.

Samuel Schoenbaum, *William Shakespeare: A Compact Documentary Life*. New York: Oxford University Press, 1977.

Robert Speaight, *Shakespeare on the Stage*. London: Collins, 1973.

Arthur C. Sprague, *Shakespeare and the Actor's Stage Business in His Plays (1660–1905)*. Cambridge, MA: Harvard University Press, 1944.

Bert O. States, *Hamlet and the Concept of Character*. Baltimore: Johns Hopkins University Press, 1992.

Richard L. Sterne, *John Gielgud Directs Richard Burton in* Hamlet: *A Journal of Rehearsals*. New York: Random House, 1967.

Tom Stoppard, *Rosencrantz and Guildenstern Are Dead*. New York: Grove Press, 1967.

Clarice Swisher, ed., *Readings on the Tragedies of William Shakespeare*. San Diego: Greenhaven Press, 1996.

Ronald Watkins, *On Producing Shakespeare*. New York: Benjamin Blom, 1964.

Index

Picture Credits

About the Author

Classical historian and literary scholar Don Nardo has written or edited numerous books about Shakespeare's plays and characters, as well as those of Chaucer, Dickens, and other noted authors. He has acted in several productions of the Bard's plays staged by the National Shakespeare Company and other troupes, and his having both played in and written about Shakespeare's works puts him in the singular position of viewing them from two very different but complementary vantage points. Mr. Nardo lives with his wife, Christine, in Massachusetts.